Hilary Walden is a well-known cookery writer and a member of the Guild of Food Writers. A regular contributor to *Taste* and *House and Garden* magazines, she is the author of several books, including *Harrods Book of Traditional English Cooking, Cuisine Express* and *Cuisine Vivante*.

By the same author

Mixer and Blender Cooking
Casserole Cooking
Home Baking
Whitworths Rice Cookbook
Whitworths Fruit and Nut Cookbook
Healthy Eating with Whitworths
Cocktails, Punches and Cups
Cocktails
The Sweet Taste of Life
Ice-cream
Harrods Book of Traditional English Cooking
Cuisine Vivante
Cuisine Express
The Complete Book of Home Confectionery
Flowerworks
The Book of French Patisserie

HILARY WALDEN

STEAMING
COOKBOOK

GRAFTON BOOKS

A Division of the Collins Publishing Group

LONDON GLASGOW
TORONTO SYDNEY AUCKLAND

Grafton Books
A Division of the Collins Publishing Group
8 Grafton Street, London W1X 3LA

Published by Grafton Books 1990

First published in Great Britain by
William Collins Sons & Co. Ltd. 1988

Illustrations by Evie Safarewicz

A CIP catalogue record for this book
is available from the British Library

ISBN 0-586-20856-9

Printed and bound in Great Britain by
Collins, Glasgow

Set in Janson and Optima

CONTENTS

INTRODUCTION

Steaming, along with boiling, has been around for about 10,000 years, almost as long as open roasting so, in comparison, it is surprising how little it is used today, apart from in the Far East.

The Chinese, Thais and Japanese use a steamer for many of their traditional dishes, the best known of which are probably the various Chinese steamed foods, often dumplings, known collectively as *dim sum*. The Chinese use bamboo woven and latticed baskets, placed over a wok of boiling water, to partly or wholly cook many of their traditional dishes, dim sum perhaps being the most well known. The steamer is also sometimes converted into a surrogate oven by placing a closed dish inside the steaming container. Indian cuisine features a number of steamed dishes, and in southern India they use a special steamer for cooking idli, the round whitish bread or cakes made from rice that are usually served with sambal or eaten for breakfast.

In Europe, however, there seem to be few recipes for steamed foods. The Sardinians steam caciocavallo (a local cheese) strips, sprinkled with oil and oregano, until melted, and from Africa comes the steamed couscous, although most couscous in the shops is now pre-cooked. Here in Britain, for most people, steaming stops at 'stodgy' suet puddings, tasteless, colourless fish and invalid food, an appalling image which is undeserved. The fault lies with the cooks and not the cooking method.

In the prevailing atmosphere of creativity, interest in pure, healthy eating and good fresh food, the picture is now beginning to change. As the potential for exciting, tasty, attractive and inspirational dishes is realized, not only are we seeing a rise in the number and variety of new recipes centred on steaming as the cooking method, but also steaming is generally being used more for the everyday cooking of food.

There are so many possibilities for creating exciting dishes using a steamer, some of which during the course of my research came as a complete surprise – duck breasts and game, for example. Steaming is extremely versatile and has many advantages over other methods of cooking.

I have attempted to provide a wide range of recipes, none of them difficult to cook, to tempt you to try steaming. As you become more familiar with the steamer I hope you will be inspired to adapt and add your own personal touches to one of the best methods of cooking still so little explored.

HILARY WALDEN

STEAMING
'KNOW-HOW'

DEFINITION

True steaming is the cooking of food directly over a boiling liquid, usually water. However, the term is also used to describe food that is cooked inside a container, such as two plates, a covered dish or a pudding basin, or wrapped in a parcel of foil or greaseproof paper, known as cooking 'en papillote'. The container or wrapping is heated and the food inside is cooked by the transference of heat from the container or wrapping and, as the food is heated, by the steam that it produces itself.

ADVANTAGES

It was not until I started to list the advantages of steaming foods that I actually realized how many there are.

Flavour, texture and enjoyment
- The true, natural flavours of food are preserved and often enhanced.
- Foods remain moist during cooking and do not dry out should they become overcooked.
- As the food is not in direct contact with the liquid it does not become soggy.
- Foods retain their shape because they remain stationary during cooking – this is especially important for delicate foods such as fish, in particular sole and plaice, vegetables and fruit.

Nutritional
- As the food does not come into contact with the liquid, the leeching out of soluble nutrients is severely reduced.

- Steaming brings out the flavour of the food so the need for additional salt is, if not eliminated, at least reduced to a minimum.
- It is a pure method of cooking so fat and oil are unnecessary.

Versatility and variety
- There is enormous scope for flavouring, adding depth to or accentuating the natural taste of foods.
- Dishes can be varied very easily by, for example, using different herbs: the flavour of steamed chicken can be subtly altered by cooking it on a bed of tarragon, thyme, rosemary or basil.
- The steaming liquid can be used as the base for a sauce to serve with the food.

Convenience
- It is an easy-to-control method of cooking.
- Steamed food does not spoil so readily if left to cook for slightly too long.
- The temperature at which food is steamed is always the same and remains constant during the cooking, thus eliminating the problems that occur during fluctuations of an oven thermostat.
- The heat is even, all round.
- More than one food can be cooked at a time without cross contamination of flavours – and in one container if quantities are small.
- It is an economical method of cooking as larger quantities of food, including a whole meal, can be cooked over just one ring or flame in a steamer with baskets stacked on top of each other.
- This then saves space, washing up, drying up and putting away.
- Food can be laid ready in the steaming basket in advance so that when the time comes to cook the food all that is necessary is to place the filled basket on the steamer.
- Once the food is cooked it can easily be removed from the heat by lifting the entire basket off the steamer.
- There is no need to strain vegetables, which I find an absolute boon when entertaining.
- Once the food is cooked it can be kept warm easily and safely in the steaming basket, over the steamer, with the heat turned off. The oven retains heat for a long time after it has been switched off so food

overcooks quickly and dries out; food left in water becomes sodden and overcooked.

● There is no need for special equipment – food can be steamed in something as simple as a sieve or colander placed over a saucepan. On the other hand, you can invest in a large capacity electric steamer which thermostatically maintains the steaming liquid at a steady temperature.

EQUIPMENT FOR STEAMING

Metal steaming basket. Available in a number of sizes, it has solid sides and a perforated base. Graduated concentric ridges underneath allow it to fit snugly into the top of pans of different diameters and capacities and enable one basket to be placed on top of another for steaming larger amounts of foods. It can be used to cook puddings in basins and some will hold a large cauliflower or small chicken. Some models come with removable dividers or compartments, enabling quick and easy transference of food into and out of the steamer and for cooking different foods at the same time. An accompanying saucepan can usually be bought as well.

Flower steamer. An expandable basket that sits inside a pan. The sides are made of a number of perforated metal panels that are attached to the base, also perforated, by hinges so that it can be expanded or closed up to fit inside many different sizes of pans, ranging normally from 13.75–23.75 cm/5½–9½ in diameter.

A flower steamer stands on three or four legs which raise it above the level of the water in the saucepan. It sometimes has a central stem for easy lifting. The stem can be removed to steam large objects, although as only a small amount of water can fit underneath these steamers are not ideal for cooking whole joints or poultry.

Chinese lidded bamboo steamer. A round basket which sits on top of a pan, traditionally a wok. The base of the basket is woven or latticed, the sides solid. The bamboo cover, which is also usually woven, absorbs the steam, preventing it from condensing and dripping on to the food.

Bamboo steamers come in many sizes and can be fitted in as many

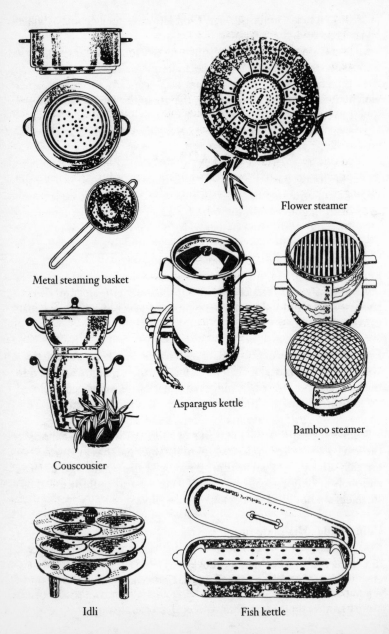

Flower steamer

Metal steaming basket

Asparagus kettle

Bamboo steamer

Couscousier

Idli

Fish kettle

tiers as you need over a saucepan or wok. If you are using a frying pan, the number of tiers is restricted to two.

The Japanese have similar wooden steamers but they are usually square or rectangular.

Improvised steamers. If you do not have proper steaming equipment, there are a number of ways in which you can improvise, although you may need to keep a closer eye on the level of the steaming liquid or make a snug-fitting cover out of foil.

You can use anything with a perforated base, that is heatproof and will fit over or can be supported inside a compatibly-sized saucepan, frying pan, Chinese wok, roasting tin or, for really large pieces of food, a preserving pan. For example:

- a colander or drum sieve
- a metal sieve (not a nylon one) for small amounts of food
- the dividing baskets from a pressure cooker
- blanching basket or chip basket
- a metal cooling rack or cake rack if the holes are not too large.

Raise the steaming container or rack above the level of the boiling water with a springform cake ring, ramekin or other heatproof dish. If the top of the steaming container has no lid or is above the level of the pan, cover it securely with foil, shaping it into a dome, if necessary, to ensure no steam escapes.

SPECIAL STEAMERS

Fish kettle. This is intended for cooking large fish such as whole salmon. The copper or aluminium lidded vessel is usually long but can be more square shaped for fish such as turbot. A rack with short legs raises the fish above the level of the water. To keep the water at a constant boil, the steamer has to be placed over two rings or burners. If you have large amounts of food to steam, a fish kettle can be the answer.

Asparagus steamer. This is not quite a true steamer because the stems of the asparagus are cooked in boiling water. The tender tips which require shorter, more delicate cooking are held above the level of the water so that they can cook more gently in the steam.

Couscousier. This is used for the traditional North African dish of couscous. The couscous is cooked in a lidded, perforated container made of earthenware, copper or, more frequently, aluminium which is then placed over a pan of liquid containing the vegetables, meat, poultry and sometimes fish.

Idli. This is a speciality of southern India and is designed to cook the dumplings made of lentils or ground rice called by the same name. It consists of three tiers with three little round hollows on each tray so that nine idli can be steamed at once. The steamer has three short legs so that it can stand in a shallow bath of boiling water inside a lidded saucepan.

TECHNIQUES AND USEFUL TIPS

Steaming is a very straightforward method of cooking and there is very little that can go wrong but there are a few simple points that should be remembered to ensure success.

● The steaming liquid must be boiling when the food is put over it.

● The container holding the food, or the pan if the sides come above the container, must be tightly covered to prevent steam from escaping as this affects the cooking time.

● Make sure that the container holding the food is well clear of the boiling water.

● Make sure there is room between the sides of the steaming vessel and the container holding the food to enable the steam to circulate.

● The water must be maintained at a constant boil although it does not have to be boiling violently – in fact, when cooking delicate egg-based dishes such as Broccoli 'Flan' (page 58) the steam must not rise too quickly.

● The level of water should be topped up with boiling water if it falls too low. Keep a kettle of boiling water, or stock, handy when steaming foods that take a long time to cook, such as steamed puddings.

● No steam should be allowed to escape. If the lid of the steamer or pan is not a good fit, or if there is no lid, use foil to seal leaking joints or as a cover.

● The food should be at room temperature, not taken straight from the refrigerator.

- To ensure even cooking, single items of food should be consistent in thickness and, if more than one piece of food is being steamed at a time, all the pieces should be the same size. On the other hand, if you want different foods to cook to different degrees vary the sizes.
- Arrange the food in a single layer, not too closely packed or touching the sides, so that the steam can circulate around the food.
- Wherever practical or possible, turn the food during cooking using tongs, a fish slice or other equipment that will not pierce the surface.
- Foods cook from the bottom (this is particularly noticeable with egg-based dishes). To slow down the cooking of the underside the food can be placed on foil or greaseproof paper.
- Protect the surface of delicate items such as Broccoli 'Flan' (page 58) and cakes and puddings from drops of condensation by laying a sheet of greaseproof paper over the surface.
- When removing the lid covering the steamed food, open it away from you to avoid a sudden rush of steam being directed towards the face.
- When open steaming and especially if the cooking is comparatively long use the steaming liquid to make an accompanying sauce as it will contain all the juices that have seeped from the food. Or save the liquid to provide the base for a sauce to serve with another food.

Cooking times in specific recipes are for those particular dishes and have taken into account any additional cooking that will take place during the time the food is being kept warm while a sauce is being made. The charts are there to help you to judge the length of time that foods should be steamed, but they are intended only as a guideline. With fish, meat, poultry and vegetables there are a number of factors that influence the cooking times and these are explained in the relevant chapters.

To keep food warm while a sauce is being prepared, or while meat is 'resting', leave the food in the steaming basket, still covered, and place this on a plate or shallow dish that will catch any juices that may seep out. Pour these juices into the sauce, towards the end of a reduction, if this is involved.

Many of the recipes include a sauce that makes use of the steaming liquid, which is often stock as this enhances the flavour of the food steamed above it and gives body and taste to a sauce. If you have no ready-made stock, make a simple, improvised version by simmering a chopped onion, carrot, leek and some fresh herbs in water and steaming the food over this. Keep some *Demi-glace* (see page 26) in the refrigerator for boosting the flavour of improvised stock.

The quantities specified for the steaming liquids in the recipes are not large. Do not boil rapidly, just maintain the liquid at boiling point. As the cooking times are not long, there should be no danger of the liquid boiling dry, although this will be affected by the diameter of the saucepan. If the level of liquid does become too low, top it up with a little more boiling water.

All the herbs that I used in the recipes were fresh. They are becoming increasingly available throughout the year and some can be grown quite easily inside in pots. However, the flavours and strength do vary, particularly during the winter months, so always sample the herbs before using them. With a little experience it is easy to assess the amount to use.

WAYS TO FLAVOUR FOOD

Steaming heightens the natural flavour of food, but it also offers many possibilities for introducing new flavours.

● Add vegetables such as carrots, onions, leeks, celery, fennel or mushrooms to the steaming liquid 15–30 minutes before steaming. This adds more flavour to the liquid and makes it more suitable for serving with the food, whether simply spooned over or made into a sauce.

● Add herbs or spices to the steaming liquid to add fragrance to the steam.

● Steam over a flavoured liquid – notably stock, perhaps, with the addition of wine, sherry, vermouth or Madeira.

● Place the food on a bed of herbs, chopped vegetables or lemon, lime or orange slices.

● Cover food with herbs, chopped vegetables or lemon, lime or orange slices.

● Marinate food in either a favourite red or white wine or a barbecue or tandoori recipe.

FOODS FOR STEAMING

The simplicity of steaming really does make the best of very fresh food so always select the highest quality food possible. In general, frozen foods do not respond to steaming as well as food that is fresh.

Rice and fresh pasta can both be cooked by steaming but I prefer to boil them partially first so that they absorb some water, swell up and become more tender.

NOTES ON THE RECIPES

In several recipes, such as Chicken on a Bed of Garlic and Parsley (page 111), where the food is flavoured directly with herbs or by a covering, the sauce that is prepared from the steaming liquid adds the final touch to the dish but is not absolutely vital. If you wish you could use just the first part of the recipe.

Whenever possible, spices were freshly ground and kept away from direct light and in a cool place for not more than three or four months.

I often use fromage blanc when making sauces because it makes a light consistency. For a richer, more creamy sauce I use whipping or double cream (except in the Fresh Coriander Sauce, page 110, which I prefer when made with fromage blanc). If you would rather use cream, simmer after adding it to thicken the sauce. The type of fromage blanc I use has 8 per cent fat (or 40 per cent *matière grasse*), unless a low-fat variety is specified.

Taste whenever you make a recipe, not just for seasoning but for the overall balance of flavours, the levels of herbs or spices and the concentration of the liquid. In savoury sauce add a little butter or cream to mellow, lemon juice to 'lift'.

BASIC RECIPES

STOCKS

There is no substitute for home-made stock. Stock cubes are too salty and cannot be used for sauces that are based upon a reduced stock.

All the stocks in this book, whether game, fish, brown veal or chicken, are easy to make and quick to prepare. But with the exception of fish stock, which takes only about 20 minutes, they do take a while to cook. However, they can be left to simmer gently during the course of an evening or at the weekend without much attention, then kept in a covered jar or bowl in the refrigerator until needed. Fish stock should be reboiled every other day, the others every three days to keep them 'sweet'.

Unless you are frequently going to use quite large amounts of stock you might find it more convenient to make a large batch then divide it and freeze it in useful measured quantities, such as 225 ml / 8 fl oz, 300 ml / ½ pint or 450 ml / 16 fl oz.

For quick 'make-do' stocks, however, I either save, and perhaps freeze, small amounts of bones and skin from cuts of meat, poultry, game or fish, or I boil them immediately with some herbs and an onion and carrot so that I have at least something with a little more character than plain water. When caught out by time, I have even steamed food over the boiling bones and skin.

For a more flavoursome liquor leave a bouquet garni of fresh Provençal herbs to infuse in veal, prepared brown veal or chicken stock while it is cooling, then remove it before freezing. Such a stock is not suitable for steaming all recipes so it is important to label it clearly.

FISH STOCK
MAKES ABOUT 1.5 LITRES / 2½ PINTS

---

20 g / ¾ oz UNSALTED BUTTER
1 ONION, CUT IN HALF
WHITE PART OF 1 LEEK, CHOPPED
50 g / 2 oz MUSHROOMS, CHOPPED
1 kg / 2 lb 2 oz FISH BONES, HEADS AND TRIMMINGS,
SOAKED IN COLD WATER FOR 3 HOURS
150 ml / ¼ PINT MEDIUM-BODIED DRY WHITE WINE
BOUQUET GARNI OF 1 BAY LEAF, 3 PARSLEY STALKS
AND SPRIG OF FENNEL

In a large saucepan, melt the butter and add the vegetables. Cover and cook over a moderate heat, shaking the pan occasionally, for 4–5 minutes. Add the fish bones, heads and trimmings and cook, stirring, for a further 2–3 minutes.

Stir in the wine, boil until reduced by half then add the bouquet garni followed by about 1.75 litres / 3 pints water. Bring to the boil, then simmer for about 25 minutes, removing the scum from the surface frequently.

Pass the stock through a sieve, lined with muslin or cheesecloth. Leave to cool then remove all the fat from the surface.

Keep the stock, covered, in the refrigerator.

CHICKEN STOCK
MAKES ABOUT 1 LITRE / 1¾ PINTS

Turkey stock can be made in the same way by using a turkey carcass
or bones.

———

1 kg / 2 lb 2 oz CHICKEN CARCASSES, NECKS, WINGS,
FEET, GIBLETS EXCEPT THE LIVER, OR 1 BOILING
FOWL, CHOPPED

1 PIG'S TROTTER OR VEAL KNUCKLE BONE,
CHOPPED

1 WHOLE ONION, SPIKED WITH 2 CLOVES

1 CARROT, SLICED

1 STICK OF CELERY, SLICED

WHITE PART OF 2 LEEKS, SLICED

BOUQUET GARNI OF 1 BAY LEAF, 4 PARSLEY STALKS,
SPRIG OF THYME AND 2 SPRIGS OF CHERVIL

———

Put the chicken carcasses, necks, wings, feet and giblets, or the boiling
fowl, and the pig's trotter, or veal bone, into a large saucepan. Add
about 2 litres / 3½ pints cold water and bring to the boil.

Carefully remove the scum from the surface, add the vegetables and
the bouquet garni. Return to the boil, then simmer for about 3 hours,
removing the scum from the surface frequently.

Pass the stock through a sieve, lined with muslin or cheesecloth, and
leave to cool. Remove the fat from the surface.

Keep the stock, covered, in the refrigerator.

GAME STOCK

MAKES ABOUT 1 LITRE/1¾ PINTS

---

1 kg/2 lb 2 oz GAME CARCASSES, BONES AND
TRIMMINGS, CHOPPED
1 TABLESPOON OIL
425 ml/15 fl oz MEDIUM-BODIED RED WINE
1 LITRE/1¾ PINTS VEAL STOCK, SEE PAGE 24
1 ONION, STUDDED WITH 2 CLOVES
1 CARROT, CHOPPED
1 STICK OF CELERY, CHOPPED
6 JUNIPER BERRIES, CRUSHED
6 CORIANDER SEEDS, CRUSHED
BOUQUET GARNI OF 1 BAY LEAF, 4 PARSLEY STALKS,
SMALL SPRIG OF SAGE AND SPRIG OF THYME

Set the oven to 220°C/425°F (gas mark 7) or turn on the grill.

Put the game carcasses, bones and trimmings into a roasting tin, pour in the oil and turn the bones to coat them lightly. Place in the oven or under the grill until lightly browned.

Tip the contents of the roasting tin into a large saucepan. Place the roasting tin over a moderate heat. Stir in the wine to dislodge the sediment, then boil until reduced to 300 ml/½ pint. Pour into the saucepan of game bones and add the stock. Bring to the boil. Remove the scum from the surface, add the remaining ingredients and simmer for 3–4 hours, or until the liquid is reduced to 1 litre/1¾ pints, removing the scum from the surface frequently.

Pass the stock through a sieve, lined with muslin or cheesecloth, then leave to cool. Remove the fat from the surface.

Keep the stock, covered, in the refrigerator.

LAMB STOCK

MAKES ABOUT 600 ml / 1 PINT

2 TABLESPOONS OIL
1 CARROT, CHOPPED
1 ONION, CHOPPED
1 STICK OF CELERY, CHOPPED
3 BLACK PEPPERCORNS
BOUQUET GARNI OF 1 BAY LEAF, 3 PARSLEY STALKS,
SPRIG OF THYME AND SMALL SPRIG OF ROSEMARY
1 kg / 2 lb 2 oz LAMB BONES

In a large saucepan, heat the oil, add the carrot, onion and celery and cook over a moderate heat, stirring occasionally, until lightly browned and softened.

Cover with 2 litres / 3½ pints cold water, add the peppercorns and bring to the boil. Remove the scum from the surface, add the bouquet garni and lamb bones. Simmer for 35–40 minutes, removing the scum occasionally.

Pass the stock through a sieve, lined with muslin or cheesecloth, and boil, if necessary, to reduce to 600 ml / 1 pint. Leave to cool, then remove the fat from the surface.

Keep the stock, covered, in the refrigerator.

VEAL STOCK
MAKES ABOUT 1 LITRE / 1¾ PINTS

---

1 kg/2 lb 2 oz VEAL KNUCKLE BONES, CHOPPED
1 ONION, STUDDED WITH A CLOVE
1 CARROT, CHOPPED
1 STICK OF CELERY, CHOPPED
WHITE PART OF 1 LEEK, CHOPPED
BOUQUET GARNI OF 1 BAY LEAF, 3 PARSLEY STALKS,
SPRIG OF THYME AND SPRIG OF CHERVIL

Blanch the veal bones for 1 minute. Drain, rinse in cold water then place in a large saucepan. Cover with about 2 litres/3½ pints cold water, bring to the boil and remove the scum from the surface.

Add the vegetables and bouquet garni. Simmer for 3–4 hours or until the liquid is reduced to about 1 litre/1¾ pints, removing the scum from the surface frequently.

Pass the stock through a sieve, lined with muslin or cheesecloth, then leave to cool. Remove the fat from the surface.

Keep the stock, covered, in the refrigerator.

BROWN VEAL STOCK
MAKES ABOUT 1 LITRE/1¾ PINTS

---

1 kg/2 lb 2 oz VEAL KNUCKLE BONES AND TRIMMINGS, CHOPPED

1 TABLESPOON OIL

1 ONION, SLICED

1 CARROT, SLICED

WHITE PART OF 1 LEEK, SLICED

1 STICK OF CELERY, SLICED

115 g/4 oz MUSHROOM TRIMMINGS

150 ml/¼ PINT MEDIUM-BODIED DRY WHITE WINE

450 g/1 lb TOMATOES, CHOPPED

BOUQUET GARNI OF 1 BAY LEAF, 4 PARSLEY STALKS, SPRIG OF THYME AND SPRIG OF TARRAGON

Set the oven to 220°C/425°F (gas mark 7) or turn on the grill.

Place the bones and trimmings into a roasting tin, pour in the oil and turn the bones so they are lightly coated. Bake in the oven or under the grill until lightly browned, turning the bones frequently.

Stir in the onion, carrot, leek and celery and return to the oven for about 10 minutes until lightly browned. Add the mushroom trimmings.

Tip the contents of the roasting tin into a large saucepan. Place the roasting tin over a moderate heat, stir in the wine to dislodge the sediment, then boil until reduced by half. Pour into the saucepan of veal bones and vegetables, and add the tomatoes, bouquet garni and about 2 litres/3½ pints cold water. Bring to the boil, remove the scum from the surface and simmer gently for 3–4 hours, or until the liquid is reduced to about 1 litre/1¾ pints.

Pass the stock through a sieve, lined with muslin or cheesecloth, and leave to cool. Remove the fat from the surface.

Keep the stock, covered, in the refrigerator.

DEMI-GLACE or MEAT GLAZE

Boil Brown Veal Stock slowly, pouring it into progressively smaller and smaller pans until it is reduced to a thick, syrupy consistency.

VEGETABLE STOCK

MAKES ABOUT 1 LITRE/1¾ PINTS

---

25 g/1 oz UNSALTED BUTTER
2 SHALLOTS, FINELY CHOPPED
WHITE PART OF 1 LEEK, FINELY CHOPPED
1 SMALL CARROT, FINELY CHOPPED
2 TABLESPOONS FINELY CHOPPED FENNEL OR
1 TEASPOON FENNEL SEEDS
2 TOMATOES, CHOPPED
BOUQUET GARNI OF 4 PARSLEY STALKS, 1 BAY LEAF,
SPRIG OF CHERVIL AND SPRIG OF THYME
1 TEASPOON WHITE PEPPERCORNS

In a large saucepan, melt the butter, add the shallots and leek, cover and cook over a low heat, shaking the pan occasionally, until softened.

Stir in the remaining ingredients, cover with 1.2 litres/2¼ pints cold water and bring to the boil. Simmer for about 20 minutes, removing the scum from the surface frequently.

Pass the stock through a sieve lined with muslin or cheesecloth, then leave to cool. Remove the fat from the surface.

Keep the stock, covered, in the refrigerator.

HOLLANDAISE SAUCE
MAKES ABOUT 300 ml/½ PINT

---

1 TABLESPOON LEMON JUICE OR WHITE WINE
VINEGAR
1 TEASPOON CRUSHED BLACK PEPPERCORNS
1 BLADE OF MACE
2 EGG YOLKS, BEATEN
175 g/6 oz UNSALTED BUTTER, MELTED
SALT
LEMON JUICE

In a small saucepan, boil the lemon juice or vinegar, peppercorns and
mace with 2 tablespoons water until reduced to 1 tablespoon. Remove
from the heat, take out the peppercorns and mace, then beat in the egg
yolks.

Place the saucepan in a larger saucepan of hot water and beat the
mixture with a wire whisk, making sure you reach into the corners,
until the mixture becomes very creamy. Check that the temperature of
the eggs does not exceed 60°C/140°F, or make sure that the temperature of the water does not reach simmering point. Gradually add the
butter, whisking constantly. As the sauce begins to thicken the butter
can be added a little more quickly. Season with salt and lemon juice.

Should the sauce curdle, add an ice cube and whisk furiously, over
the water, until it becomes smooth again. Remove the ice cube
immediately.

BLENDER HOLLANDAISE

This is easier and quicker to make than the traditional version but
should please all but the severest critics.

---

175 g/6 oz UNSALTED BUTTER, DICED
1 TABLESPOON LEMON JUICE OR WHITE WINE
VINEGAR

3 EGG YOLKS
SALT AND FRESHLY GROUND WHITE PEPPER
CASTER SUGAR (OPTIONAL)

In one saucepan, heat the butter until just melted, and in another pan, the lemon juice or vinegar until bubbling.

Blend the egg yolks briefly in a blender or food processor then, with the motor running, slowly trickle in the hot lemon juice or vinegar. When the mixture is well blended, still with the motor running, very slowly pour in the melted butter to give a smooth, thick, 'creamy' sauce. Season with salt and white pepper and adjust the sharpness, if necessary, with lemon juice or caster sugar.

For herb hollandaise: add approximately 2 tablespoons chopped herbs to the finished sauce. **For orange hollandaise:** use orange juice instead of lemon for the final seasoning and add the finely grated rind of 1 orange. **For ginger hollandaise:** add approximately 1 tablespoon chopped, peeled fresh root ginger to the finished sauce. **For mustard hollandaise:** add 1–2 teaspoons Dijon mustard to the finished sauce.

FIRST COURSES
AND LIGHT DISHES

A steamer is very useful for preparing first courses, light dishes and snacks easily, quickly and healthily, from warm salads and light fish dishes to egg recipes and many others that are usually cooked in a *bain-marie*, for example, Carrot Kugelhopf (page 49).

When cooking egg and egg-based dishes, steam them in individual portions or shallow containers as the underneath will set while the top is still moist. You can also even out the cooking by first lining the basket with foil or greaseproof paper.

EGGS IN TOMATOES

SERVES 4

The flavoured soft cheese is not absolutely vital but it slows down the cooking of the undersides of the eggs and leaves a delicious creamy pool beneath them.

———————

4 LARGE TOMATOES

APPROX 25 g/1 oz HERB, GARLIC OR BLACK PEPPER FLAVOURED SOFT CHEESE

4 EGGS

———————

With a sharp knife, cut a slice from the top of each tomato. Using a teaspoon, carefully scoop out the seeds and flesh, then place a small knob of flavoured cheese in the bottom.

Transfer the tomatoes to a steaming basket, colander or rack then carefully break an egg into each one. Replace the tomato tops and steam for about 15 minutes until the egg yolks are just set, or longer if firmer yolks are preferred.

ROLLED OMELETTE WITH GOATS' CHEESE AND BASIL

SERVES 1

Omelettes are easy to make in a steaming basket. Line the bottom of the basket with a sheet of greaseproof paper and simply pour on a thin layer of beaten eggs. Steam for about 2 minutes. And, what's more, you can determine the shape of the omelette by the way the greaseproof paper is folded.

---

50 g/2 oz GOATS' CHEESE, FINELY CHOPPED
APPROX 1 TABLESPOON FROMAGE FRAIS
2 EGGS
1 TABLESPOON MILK
SALT AND FRESHLY GROUND BLACK PEPPER
APPROX 1½ TABLESPOONS FINELY SHREDDED BASIL

Work together the goats' cheese and the fromage frais and put to one side. Beat the eggs with the milk and season lightly with salt and pepper.

Line a steaming basket or rack with a sheet of lightly buttered or oiled greaseproof paper. Fold up the edges of the paper to make a rectangle approximately 12.5 × 17.5 cm/5 × 7 in. When the water in the steamer is boiling, pour the beaten egg mixture into the paper, making sure it is distributed evenly over the surface. Cover and steam for about 2 minutes – the underside should be set but the top still slightly liquid.

Remove the basket or rack from the heat, sprinkle the basil evenly over the surface and lift the omelette, with the paper, using a fish slice, if necessary, to support it underneath.

Sprinkle the top of the omelette with the cheese, then with the help of the paper, roll the omelette up like a Swiss roll.

To serve, either cut into slices with a sharp knife, or leave as a roll.

'POACHED' EGGS ON A VEGETABLE NEST

SERVES 1

Although this recipe serves only one, the number of portions can easily be increased, if the steaming basket is large enough.

---

115 g/4 oz MIXED VEGETABLES E.G. LEEKS, CARROTS, CELERY, COURGETTES, CUT INTO FINE STRIPS
SALT AND FRESHLY GROUND BLACK PEPPER
HERB HOLLANDAISE, SEE PAGE 28

Line the bottom of a steaming basket or colander with a sheet of greaseproof paper and place a lightly buttered pastry cutter, poaching ring or crumpet ring on top. Break the egg into the ring, cover with another piece of greaseproof paper and cook the egg for about 7 minutes, until the top is just beginning to set – the egg cooks from underneath so although the top still appears moist the base will be set.

Just before the egg is cooked, place the vegetables around the outside of the ring. Steam for 1–2 minutes so that they remain crisp.

To serve, transfer the vegetables to a plate and form into a 'nest'. Season lightly with salt and pepper. Using a fish slice, lift the egg, still on the greaseproof paper, from the steaming vessel. Remove the ring, ease the egg off the paper and slip it on to the 'nest'. If preferred, the egg can be inverted. Spoon a little of the Hollandaise over the egg and serve the rest separately.

SAVOURY BREAD PUDDINGS

SERVES 4

12 THIN CIRCLES OF BREAD TO FIT INSIDE RAMEKIN
DISHES APPROXIMATELY 7.5–8 cm/3–3½ in IN
DIAMETER

BUTTER

WHOLEGRAIN OR MEAUX MUSTARD

50 g/2 oz THINLY SLICED HAM, FAT REMOVED,
CHOPPED

50 g/2 oz MATURE CHEDDAR CHEESE, FINELY
GRATED

2 EGGS, BEATEN

300 ml/½ PINT MILK OR SINGLE CREAM, OR HALF
MILK/HALF CREAM

SALT AND FRESHLY GROUND BLACK PEPPER

SPRIGS OF FRESH HERBS, SUCH AS PARSLEY OR
CHERVIL, FOR GARNISH

A COLOURFUL SAUCE, SUCH AS RED PEPPER SAUCE
(SEE PAGE 183) TO SERVE (OPTIONAL)

Spread the bread with butter and mustard then place 1 circle in each of 4 well-buttered, approximately 185 ml/6½ fl oz ramekin dishes. Divide the ham and cheese into 2 portions each then divide one half of each between the ramekins. Cover with another circle of bread and scatter the remaining ham and cheese over. Beat the eggs and milk or cream lightly together, add pepper and a little salt then strain into the dishes. Leave to stand for about an hour then place a piece of greaseproof paper lightly over the tops of the dishes and steam for 30 minutes until just set. Leave to stand for a few minutes before unmoulding onto warmed plates. Place a fresh herb sprig on the top of each pudding for garnish. Spoon the sauce around, if used.

TROUT IN PAPER PURSES
SERVES 4

Serve these parcels closed so that everyone can enjoy the wonderful herby aromas that waft up as the paper is opened.

---

200 g/7 oz TROUT FILLET, SKINNED AND CUT INTO
1.25 cm/½ in CUBES
1 TABLESPOON CHOPPED PARSLEY
4 TEASPOONS CHOPPED MINT
SCANT ½ TEASPOON FENNEL SEEDS
45 g/1¾ oz FINELY DICED RED PEPPER
SALT AND FRESHLY GROUND BLACK PEPPER
3 TABLESPOONS LIME OR LEMON JUICE
3 TABLESPOONS DRY WHITE VERMOUTH
25 g/1 oz UNSALTED BUTTER, MELTED (OPTIONAL)

Lightly toss together the trout, herbs, red pepper, salt and black pepper. Divide the mixture into 4 and place each portion in the centre of a sheet of greaseproof paper, approximately 25 cm/10 in square. Sprinkle with the lime or lemon juice, vermouth, and melted butter, if used. Fold up the corners of the greaseproof paper to meet in the middle over the trout mixture and twist them together to seal. Steam for about 2½–3 minutes.

Serve the parcels unopened on warmed plates.

WARM SCALLOP AND JERUSALEM ARTICHOKE SALAD

SERVES 4

If you have time, this salad looks particularly attractive if the slices of artichoke and scallop are arranged in neat, slightly overlapping circles.

---

900 g/2 lb JERUSALEM ARTICHOKES
1 TABLESPOON LEMON JUICE
8–12 SCALLOPS, DEPENDING ON SIZE
1 HEAD OF CURLY ENDIVE
8 BASIL LEAVES, SHREDDED
40 g/1½ oz PINE NUTS

DRESSING
1 TABLESPOON HAZELNUT OIL
4 TABLESPOONS OLIVE OIL
1–2 TABLESPOONS WHITE WINE VINEGAR
1 TEASPOON WHOLEGRAIN MUSTARD
SALT AND FRESHLY GROUND BLACK PEPPER

Mix together all the ingredients for the dressing and put to one side.

Peel the Jerusalem artichokes and cut into approximately 1.25 cm/½ in slices. Toss the slices in the lemon juice then steam for about 6 minutes, until just tender.

Meanwhile, separate the scallop corals from the bodies and cut the bodies horizontally into halves or 3 slices, depending on size. Lay the corals and slices on a cloth to dry.

Remove the artichoke slices from the steaming vessel and keep warm. Steam the scallop bodies and corals for 45–60 seconds.

To serve, arrange the curly endive in a circle, place the slices of artichoke in a circle on top of the endive, then lay the scallop bodies in a circle inside the artichokes. The scallop corals go in the centre.

Add the basil to the dressing then sprinkle it over the artichokes and scallops. Finish with a scattering of pine nuts.

SCALLOP DIM SUM
WITH HERB DIP

MAKES ABOUT 14

My western version of a dumpling-type of dim sum is made with a thinner dough than its Chinese counterparts and so cooks more quickly, tastes much lighter, and can be filled with more delicate ingredients. As an alternative to scallops, try diced raw prawns as a filling.

100 g/3½ oz PLAIN FLOUR
FRESHLY GROUND WHITE PEPPER
1 TABLESPOON FINELY CHOPPED FRESH FENNEL
225 g/8 oz SCALLOP BODIES, CUT INTO
1.25 cm/½ in CUBES
1½ TEASPOONS FINELY GRATED LEMON RIND
3 TABLESPOONS FROMAGE FRAIS

HERB DIP
1 LARGE SPRING ONION, CHOPPED
PINCH OF SEA SALT
50 ml/2 fl oz THICK GREEK YOGHURT
75 g/3 oz FROMAGE FRAIS
FRESHLY GROUND WHITE PEPPER

APPROX 3 TABLESPOONS CHOPPED MIXED HERBS,
E.G. CHIVES, PARSLEY,
CHERVIL AND TARRAGON

Mix the flour, pepper and fennel with 50 ml/2 fl oz warm water to make a dough, then knead for about 3 minutes on a very lightly floured surface. Cover with a warmed upturned bowl and leave for about 30 minutes.

Meanwhile, lightly mix the scallops with the lemon rind and fromage frais and put to one side.

Form the dough into a roll, then cut into 16 slices. Flatten each piece out to a thin circle, measuring about 9 cm/3½ in diameter. Divide the scallop mixture between the circles, dampen the edges with water and fold them up to form balls.

Line a steaming basket, colander or rack with a cloth, arrange the dumplings on top and place over a saucepan of gently boiling water. Cover with a lid and steam for 7 minutes.

For the dip, in a mortar crush to a paste the spring onion with a little sea salt. Fold the yoghurt into the fromage frais, then gradually work in the spring onion paste. Add freshly ground white pepper and herbs to taste. Transfer to a bowl and serve as a dip for the dim sum.

PRAWN AND SOLE
BALLS

SERVES 4

I am very fond of these light, delicate mouthfuls. On a plate, garnished with a few crisp lettuce leaves, they are one of my favourite first courses. In summer, accompanied by a crisp salad and French bread, I think they make an ideal light lunch.

Chive mustard is one of the increasing number of flavoured mustards now commercially available.

115 g/4 oz COOKED AND SHELLED PRAWNS
115 g/4 oz SOLE FILLET, SKINNED
1½ TABLESPOONS LEMON JUICE
½ AN EGG WHITE
SALT AND FRESHLY GROUND BLACK PEPPER
2 TABLESPOONS FINELY CHOPPED CHIVES
1 TEASPOON CHIVE MUSTARD
LONG STRIP OF LEMON RIND
300 ml/½ PINT FISH STOCK, SEE PAGE 20
3 TABLESPOONS DRY WHITE VERMOUTH
(OPTIONAL)
115 ml/4 fl oz CRÈME FRAÎCHE OR WHIPPING CREAM

Purée together the prawns and sole, or pass through a sieve. Mix in the lemon juice, egg white and season with salt and pepper. Add the chives and mustard. Divide the mixture into 16 small balls, place them between absorbent kitchen paper and chill lightly.

Add the lemon rind to the fish stock. Place the balls in a steaming basket or colander or on a rack lined with greaseproof paper and steam over the stock for 3 minutes. Remove from the heat and keep warm.

Add the vermouth, if used, to the stock, and boil until it becomes slightly syrupy, then whisk in the crème fraîche or whipping cream.

Serve the fish balls with the sauce poured around.

BASIL-WRAPPED PRAMS
BASIL-WRAPPED PRAWNS

SERVES 4

---

12 LARGE MEDITERRANEAN PRAWNS
SQUEEZE OF LEMON JUICE
SALT AND FRESHLY GROUND BLACK PEPPER
APPROX 36 LARGE BASIL LEAVES
4 LEMON WEDGES

Peel the prawns, but leave on the tails. Carefully remove and discard the dark digestive tracts. Sprinkle a little lemon juice over each prawn and season lightly. Wrap the body of each prawn in basil leaves, then steam for 2 minutes.

Carefully lift from the steaming vessel, keeping the basil leaves in place, and serve with a wedge of lemon.

SARDINES WITH SEAWEED

SERVES 4

If fresh sardines are not available, frozen ones can be used for this dish. Wakame is a Japanese dried seaweed available from good supermarkets and speciality shops. However, shredded spinach and sorrel leaves can be used instead.

---

20 g/¾ oz WAKAME, SOAKED FOR 5 MINUTES
8 FRESH SARDINES, GUTTED, CLEANED AND
SCALED, BUT HEADS AND TAILS LEFT ON
FRESHLY GROUND BLACK PEPPER
4 TABLESPOONS LEMON JUICE

Squeeze the water from the wakame and use half the amount to cover the bottom of a steaming basket or colander or a rack. Lay the sardines on top, sprinkle with black pepper, then cover with the remaining wakame. Steam for 4–5 minutes.

Meanwhile, warm the lemon juice.

To serve, make a bed out of the wakame, lay the sardines on top and sprinkle with the lemon juice.

HADDOCK PASTA ROLLS WITH CHIVE SAUCE

SERVES 4

4 SHEETS DRIED GREEN LASAGNE, EACH MEASURING ABOUT 7.5 × 17.5 cm/3 × 7 in

½ A SMALL ONION, FINELY CHOPPED

50 g/2 oz SOFT CHEESE WITH GARLIC AND HERBS

225 g/8 oz HADDOCK FILLET, SKINNED AND CHOPPED

1 SMALL EGG, BEATEN

SALT AND FRESHLY GROUND BLACK PEPPER

20 g/¾ oz CHIVES, CHOPPED

100 ml/3½ fl oz VEGETABLE STOCK OR MILK

225 g/8 oz FROMAGE BLANC

LEMON JUICE

CHIVE FLOWERS OR SHORT STRIPS OF CHIVE FOR GARNISH

Boil the lasagne for 5 minutes. Drain well then lay the sheets in a folded tea towel to dry.

Mix together the onion, cheese, haddock, egg, salt and pepper. Then, either in a food processor or blender or by passing through a sieve, purée until smooth. Spread this mixture out evenly on each piece of lasagne. Roll up tightly and wrap separately in lightly oiled, seasoned foil. Steam for about 8 minutes.

Meanwhile, purée half of the chives in the stock or milk. Mix in the fromage blanc. Add the remaining chives. Season to taste with salt, black pepper and lemon juice. Open the foil surrounding each pasta roll and, using a sharp knife, cut each roll into 6 slices.

To serve, pour the sauce on to 4 warmed plates and arrange the pasta rolls on top. Garnish with chive flowers or short strips of chive.

SMALL SQUID FILLED WITH PARSLEY AND MUSHROOMS

SERVES 4–6

I would always recommend using small squid as they are so much more tender, delicately flavoured, and require less cooking than large ones.

12 SMALL SQUID, TOTAL WEIGHT ABOUT 700 g/1½ lb
6 TABLESPOONS FINELY CHOPPED PARSLEY
50 g/2 oz LARGE CUP MUSHROOMS, FINELY CHOPPED
1 SMALL ONION, FINELY CHOPPED
SALT AND FRESHLY GROUND BLACK PEPPER
1 TOMATO, SKINNED AND SEEDS REMOVED,
CHOPPED
½ AN EGG WHITE
2 LARGE CLOVES OF GARLIC, SPLIT
FISH STOCK FOR STEAMING (OPTIONAL),
SEE PAGE 20
SMALL SPRIGS OF PARSLEY FOR GARNISH

TOMATO SAUCE
1 SHALLOT, FINELY CHOPPED
1 CLOVE OF GARLIC, FINELY CRUSHED
15 g/½ oz UNSALTED BUTTER
575 g/1¼ lb RIPE TOMATOES, SKINNED AND CHOPPED
1 BAY LEAF
1 SPRIG EACH OF PARSLEY AND THYME
SALT AND FRESHLY GROUND BLACK PEPPER
1 TEASPOON CHOPPED BASIL
½ TEASPOON CHOPPED TARRAGON

Pull the head and tentacles of the squid away from the body, drawing the insides out at the same time. Discard the insides. Chop and reserve the tentacles. Draw out and discard the fine backbone, then rinse the remaining body pouch in cold running water. Drain well.

Mix together the tentacles, parsley, mushrooms, onion, salt, pepper, tomato and egg white, and divide between the squid bodies. Sew up the openings loosely.

Add the garlic cloves to the fish stock or seasoned water. Line a steaming basket or colander with a sheet of greaseproof paper, lay the squid on top and steam for about 50 minutes.

Meanwhile, prepare the sauce. Cook the shallot and garlic gently in the butter, until softened but not coloured. Add the tomatoes, bay leaf,

parsley and thyme, and simmer gently for about 10 minutes, stirring occasionally. Sieve, return to the saucepan and add the seasoning. Add the chopped herbs, cover and leave to infuse for 10 minutes or so.

Cut the squid into slices, garnish with small sprigs of parsley and serve with the warm sauce.

COURGETTE, CHERVIL AND SMOKED SALMON SOUFFLÉS

SERVES 4

It is important to use small, young courgettes as older, larger ones contain too much moisture.

---

4 THIN SLICES OF SMOKED SALMON
115 g/ 4 oz SMALL COURGETTES, FINELY GRATED
175 g/6 oz RICOTTA CHEESE, SIEVED
APPROX 1 TABLESPOON FINELY CHOPPED CHERVIL
SALT AND FRESHLY GROUND BLACK PEPPER
2 EGG WHITES

Line four approximately 150 g/5 oz ramekin dishes with the smoked salmon.

Pat the courgettes with absorbent kitchen paper to remove any excess moisture. Mix together with the ricotta cheese and chervil, and season with black pepper and very little salt.

Whisk the egg whites until stiff but not dry, then lightly fold into the ricotta mixture. Divide between the dishes and steam for about 8 minutes, until lightly set in the centre. Serve immediately.

KING PRAWNS FILLED WITH MONKFISH

SERVES 4

If you like Chinese food, you could replace the Tabasco in this
recipe with soy sauce.

---

200 g/7 oz MONKFISH, MINCED

TABASCO SAUCE

8 KING PRAWNS, SHELLS AND TAILS INTACT

FISH STOCK FOR STEAMING (OPTIONAL),
SEE PAGE 20

SPRING ONION, VERY FINELY CHOPPED,
FOR GARNISH

Season the monkfish with a little Tabasco. Remove the heads and legs
from the prawns. Split the bodies lengthways along their undersides,
but do not cut right through. Divide the monkfish into 8 and form
each portion into a small 'finger'. Place inside the prawns, then steam
over the fish stock, or water seasoned with sea salt and black pepper,
for about 2 minutes.

Garnish the monkfish with the spring onion. Serve the prawns with
paper napkins and use small forks for removing the flesh from the
shells.

JAPANESE CHICKEN AND PRAWN CUSTARDS

SERVES 4

Savoury steamed custard, containing both white meat and fish, is a
very popular dish in Japan. The consistency is much thinner than
that of normal Western custard. Dashi is a stock used in Japanese
cooking, made from dried bonito fish flakes and konbu seaweed. If
neither the ingredients nor ready-made dashi are available, a chicken
stock can be used instead.

---

4 RAW PRAWNS, SHELLED, DEVEINED AND HALVED
LENGTHWAYS

SEA SALT

½ CHICKEN BREAST, SKINNED AND CUT INTO
1.25 cm/1½ in PIECES

FEW DROPS OF SAKE (OPTIONAL)

SHIITAKE MUSHROOMS, CHOPPED

450 ml/16 fl oz DASHI OR CHICKEN STOCK, SEE PAGE 21

4 EGGS, LIGHTLY BEATEN

½ TEASPOON JAPANESE SOY SAUCE

4 YOUNG SPINACH LEAVES

Sprinkle the prawns with a little sea salt, the chicken with a little sake,
if desired. Then divide the prawns, chicken and mushrooms between
four 225 ml/8 fl oz heatproof bowls.

Mix together the dashi, or chicken stock, eggs and soy sauce, then
divide between the bowls. Float a spinach leaf on top of each. Cover
the bowls with foil, then steam for 10–12 minutes, until the custard
has set very lightly.

HERBED CHICKEN LIVERS WITH RED WINE SAUCE

SERVES 4

---

450 g/1 lb CHICKEN LIVERS, CUT INTO STRIPS
175 ml/6 fl oz MILK
1 TABLESPOON CHOPPED TARRAGON
1 TABLESPOON CHOPPED PARSLEY
1 TABLESPOON CHOPPED CHERVIL
SALT AND FRESHLY GROUND BLACK PEPPER
300 ml/½ PINT CHICKEN STOCK, SEE PAGE 21
225 ml/8 fl oz MEDIUM-BODIED DRY WHITE WINE
50 g/2 oz UNSALTED BUTTER, DICED
SPRIGS OF CHERVIL, FOR GARNISH

Soak the livers in the milk for an hour. Drain and dry on absorbent kitchen paper. Toss them in the herbs, salt and pepper to coat. Arrange in a single layer on the bottom of a steaming basket or colander and steam over the stock and wine for about 5 minutes, so that the insides of the strips remain very pink. Remove the basket or colander from the pan and keep the liver warm.

To make the sauce, boil the steaming liquid rapidly until reduced to 150 ml/¼ pint. Add any juices that have seeped out of the liver, then lower the heat and gradually swirl in the butter, making sure each piece is incorporated before adding the next. Adjust the seasoning, if necessary.

Serve the liver with the sauce poured over and garnish with sprigs of chervil.

CARROT KUGELHOPF

SERVES 4

An Orange or Ginger Hollandaise Sauce (see page 28) rounds this dish off to perfection.

---

450 g/1 lb YOUNG CARROTS, TRIMMED AND
THINLY SLICED

4 EGGS

50 ml/2 fl oz CRÈME FRAÎCHE OR DOUBLE CREAM

1½ TABLESPOONS LEMON JUICE

SALT AND FRESHLY GROUND BLACK PEPPER

300 ml/½ PINT ORANGE OR GINGER HOLLANDAISE
SAUCE

1 LEEK, CUT INTO THIN STRIPS, FOR GARNISH

Weigh out three-quarters of the carrots then steam for 3 minutes, until tender. Purée with the eggs, crème fraîche, or double cream, and lemon juice. Season to taste. Divide the mixture between 4 buttered individual ring moulds. Cover the tops of the moulds loosely with greaseproof paper. Lay a double thickness of greaseproof paper in a steaming basket or on a rack, place the ring moulds on top and steam for 6–7 minutes, until just set. Remove the moulds and leave to stand for a minute or so.

In the meantime, prepare the Orange or Ginger Hollandaise Sauce.

Steam the reserved carrot slices for about 2 minutes and the strips of leek for 1 minute so that both vegetables remain crisp.

Turn out the carrot kugelhopf and pour the sauce around – a thin trail can also be trickled over the top. Garnish with the carrot slices and strips of leek.

HOT/COLD FILLED AVOCADOS

SERVES 4

I am not a fan of hot avocados but this method of serving them –
halved, steamed and still in their skins – seems to give them a very
different flavour. Pesto sauce is a Mediterranean basil and pine nut
sauce, and can be made at home or bought ready-prepared.
Alternatively, the fromage frais can be flavoured with a few drops of
Tabasco or horseradish sauce.

---

2 JUST RIPE AVOCADOS, WEIGHING ABOUT 250 g/9 oz
EACH, HALVED AND STONED
115 g/4 oz FROMAGE FRAIS
APPROX 1 TEASPOON PESTO SAUCE
115 g/4 oz SHELLED PRAWNS, CHOPPED
BASIL LEAVES, FOR GARNISH

Steam the avocados for about 7–8 minutes.
  Meanwhile, flavour the fromage frais with pesto sauce and stir in
the prawns. Divide the prawn mixture equally between the avocados,
garnish with the basil leaves and serve immediately.

WARM FENNEL
MOUSSES
SERVES 6

This very light mixture rises well during cooking and you may prefer
to serve it in the ramekin dishes. If so, serve immediately as the
mousse soon sinks.

---

250 g/9 oz FLORENCE FENNEL BULB, TRIMMED
AND SLICED

75 g/3 oz FROMAGE FRAIS

SALT AND FRESHLY GROUND BLACK PEPPER

2 EGG WHITES

Steam the fennel for 5–6 minutes, until very tender. Then purée with
the fromage frais. Season with salt and pepper.

Whisk the egg whites until stiff, but not dry, then lightly fold into
the fennel purée. Divide between six buttered 115–150 g/4–5 oz
ramekin dishes. Lay a sheet of greaseproof paper in a steaming basket
or on a rack, place the ramekin dishes on top and steam for about 6–7
minutes, until well risen and just set.

Remove from the heat and leave to stand for a few minutes before
inverting on to warmed plates.

CELERIAC WITH
STILTON AND WALNUTS
SERVES 4

---

350 g/12 oz PARED CELERIAC, CUT INTO
1.25 cm/½ in DICE
2 EGG YOLKS
SALT AND FRESHLY GROUND BLACK PEPPER
100 g/3½ oz STILTON CHEESE, ROUGHLY CRUMBLED
4 TABLESPOONS CHOPPED WALNUTS

Steam the celeriac for 7–8 minutes, until soft, then purée with the egg yolks, salt and pepper.

Use about three-quarters of this mixture to line evenly four 125 ml/4½ fl oz greased ramekin dishes. Mix together the cheese and nuts, then divide between the ramekin dishes. Cover with the remaining celeriac mixture. Place a piece of greaseproof paper lightly on top then steam for 5–6 minutes.

Run the point of a sharp knife carefully around the edges of the moulds to loosen and turn out on to warmed plates.

MIXED VEGETABLES
WITH NUT SAUCE DIP

SERVES 4–6

The vegetables can be varied according to availability and personal
preference, but try to aim for a variety of textures, colours and
flavours.

---

350 ml/12 fl oz VEGETABLE STOCK, SEE PAGE 26

115 g/4 oz CAULIFLOWER FLORETS, DIVIDED INTO
SMALL SPRIGS

115 g/4 oz CARROTS, CUT INTO STRIPS

115 g/4 oz COURGETTES, CUT INTO STRIPS

BUNCH OF SPRING ONIONS, TRIMMED

12 BUTTON MUSHROOMS, SLICED

1 SMALL ONION, FINELY CHOPPED

2 CLOVES OF GARLIC, FINELY CRUSHED

½–1 TEASPOON CHILLI POWDER

1 TEASPOON SOFT BROWN SUGAR

JUICE OF 1 LARGE LIME

25 g/1 oz CREAMED COCONUT, ROUGHLY CHOPPED

115g/4 oz UNSALTED PEANUTS, ROASTED IN THE
OVEN THEN GROUND

SALT AND FRESHLY GROUND BLACK PEPPER

FRESH CORIANDER, FOR GARNISH

Steam the cauliflower over the stock for about 8 minutes, the carrots
for about 7, the courgettes for 2, the spring onions for 2–3 depending
on size, and the mushrooms for about 2. All the vegetables should
remain crisp. Keep the vegetables warm.

Steam the chopped onion and the garlic for about 3 minutes, until
soft. Transfer to a small saucepan, stir in the chilli powder and about 1
tablespoon of the stock. Cook, stirring with a wooden spoon, for 1–2

minutes, then stir in the remaining stock followed by the sugar, lime juice and creamed coconut. Bring to the boil, stirring. Finally, stir in the ground peanuts, then simmer for about 15–20 minutes until thickened. Taste, season and adjust the flavourings if necessary.

Pour into a warmed bowl, garnish with fresh coriander and serve on a platter with the vegetables arranged neatly around.

WHOLE STUFFED COURGETTES

SERVES 4

---

4 COURGETTES, APPROX 10 cm/4 in LONG
100 g/3½ oz LEAN HAM, MINCED
2 TABLESPOONS FINELY CHOPPED CHIVES
2 TABLESPOONS FINELY CHOPPED PARSLEY
1 TABLESPOON FINELY CHOPPED THYME
1 TABLESPOON LEMON JUICE
DASH OF TABASCO SAUCE
SALT AND FRESHLY GROUND BLACK PEPPER
1 EGG, BEATEN

Push an apple corer through each courgette to hollow out the seeds. Mix together the ham, herbs, lemon juice, Tabasco, salt and pepper, then add enough egg to bind the mixture.

Carefully fill the hollowed-out courgettes then steam for about 25 minutes.

COURGETTE FLOWERS
AND COURGETTES

SERVES 4

Limited supplies of young courgettes with their flowers attached are available from specialist greengrocers.

---

4 FINGER-SIZED COURGETTES WITH THEIR
FLOWERS
115g/4 oz MONKFISH FILLET
SALT
SQUEEZE OF LEMON JUICE
1 EGG WHITE
150 ml/¼ PINT DOUBLE CREAM
2 TEASPOONS DRY WHITE VERMOUTH
FRESHLY GROUND WHITE PEPPER
FRESHLY GRATED NUTMEG
400 ml/14 fl oz VEGETABLE STOCK, SEE PAGE 26
150 ml/¼ PINT CRÈME FRAÎCHE
50 g/2 oz FRESH PRAWNS, SHELLED
SPRIGS OF DILL OR FENNEL, FOR GARNISH

Very gently remove the flowers from the courgettes. Purée, either in a food processor or blender or by rubbing through a sieve, the monkfish with the salt until smooth. Add a squeeze of lemon juice and the egg white and purée again until stiff. Gradually beat in the cream and vermouth to give a softish, pipeable mousse and season with freshly ground white pepper and nutmeg.

Spoon this mixture into a piping bag, fitted with a fairly small plain nozzle, and very carefully fill each flower about half full. Tuck the ends of the petals over to seal in the mousse, then place each flower, with the folded ends underneath, in a steaming basket or colander. Add the courgettes and steam over the stock for 4 minutes. Remove the basket or colander from the pan and keep the courgettes and courgette flowers warm.

To make the sauce, boil the stock until reduced to 50 ml / 2 fl oz, stir in the crème fraîche and bubble until slightly thickened. Lower the heat and add the prawns to warm through. Season to taste.

Cut each courgette lengthways to make 4 slices. Spoon the sauce, without the prawns, on to warmed plates, lay the courgettes and flowers on top, then add the prawns. Garnish with sprigs of dill or fennel.

NEW POTATO CUSTARD CUPS
MAKES 6

Serve as canapés, *amuse gueles* or as a first course, accompanied by a small green salad. The scooped-out balls of flesh are ideal for serving on cocktail sticks with a savoury dip.

_____

6 NEW POTATOES, WEIGHING ABOUT 25 g / 1 oz EACH

2 EGG YOLKS

75 ml / 3 fl oz SOURED CREAM OR THICK PLAIN YOGHURT

SALT AND FRESHLY GROUND BLACK PEPPER

HANDFUL OF CHIVES

CAVIARE OR SALMON EGGS OR CHIVES, FINELY CHOPPED, FOR GARNISH

_____

Using a sharp knife, cut a small slice off one side of each potato. With a melon baller or small, sharp-edged teaspoon, scoop out the flesh to leave a thin shell, taking care not to break the skin. Mix together the egg yolks and soured cream or yoghurt and season very lightly.

Lay a bed of chives in a steaming basket or colander, and place over boiling seasoned water. Place the potato shells on the chives, using some of the scooped-out potato, if necessary, to wedge them upright. Carefully spoon the soured cream or yoghurt mixture into the shells, cover and steam for about 15 minutes, until they are just tender.

Serve warm with caviare or salmon eggs or finely chopped chives sprinkled over the top.

SPINACH POLPETTES

SERVES 4–6

Steamed polpettes are much lighter and easier to cook than normal polpettes (a type of Italian dumpling) as they do not contain flour and therefore do not break up during cooking. Traditionally, they are served sprinkled with melted butter.

575 g / 1¼ lb YOUNG SPINACH, STALKS REMOVED,
LEAVES SHREDDED
175 g / 6 oz SKIMMED MILK SOFT CHEESE, SIEVED
SALT AND FRESHLY GROUND BLACK PEPPER
FRESHLY GRATED NUTMEG
1 EGG WHITE

Using a covered, wide frying pan or saucepan – nonstick is best – heat some of the spinach gently until it begins to wilt. Stir and add some more. Cover and heat again. Repeat until all of the spinach has wilted. Heat for a while with the pan uncovered to allow moisture to evaporate.

In batches again, transfer the spinach to a fine sieve and press firmly to expel as much moisture as possible. Turn the drained spinach into a bowl. Beat in the soft cheese, then season with salt, black pepper and nutmeg. Finally work in the egg white.

Using a dessert spoon, form the mixture into torpedo shapes. Line a steaming basket or colander with a sheet of greaseproof paper, place the polpettes on top and steam for about 7–8 minutes, turning over carefully about half-way through. Depending on the size of the basket or colander that you are using, it may be necessary to cook the polpettes in batches.

BROCCOLI 'FLAN'

SERVES 4

This recipe allows the pure taste of really fresh broccoli to come through but if, during steaming, the broccoli lacks flavour, add a pinch of grated nutmeg or a little mustard. For a less rich flan use all milk instead of cream. This flan is not restricted to broccoli; a similarly prepared weight of other vegetables can be used instead.

---

300 g/10 oz TRIMMED BROCCOLI FLORETS
2 EGGS
150 ml/¼ PINT SINGLE CREAM
150 ml/¼ PINT MILK
SALT AND FRESHLY GROUND BLACK PEPPER

Steam the broccoli for about 5 minutes, until very tender. Then purée with the remaining ingredients.

Pour into a lightly buttered, preferably nonstick 15 cm/6 in flan tin. Lay a double thickness of foil in a steaming basket or on a rack, place the flan tin on top and cover with a piece of greaseproof paper. Steam for about 8 minutes.

Turn the heat off and leave the flan tin in place for about another 5 minutes. Remove the tin from the basket or colander and leave to stand for 3 minutes or so.

To serve, invert the flan on to a warmed plate.

FISH AND SHELLFISH

Steaming is the most sympathetic way of cooking fish and shellfish and shows off fresh, good-quality fish to the best advantage. It is also easy, interesting and inspirational.

Steaming is particularly suitable for fish with fragile, delicate flesh, such as sole and plaice, especially completely filleted and skinned pieces. Cooking several pieces of fish so they are all done to just the right degree is no problem when they are steamed, as all the fish can be placed in the steaming basket away from the heat, placed over the steam all together, then the steaming basket simply lifted off the heat after the required length of time.

Steaming is also the ideal method for cooking molluscs and shellfish, keeping the flesh tender and full of flavour. For instance, perfect scallops steamed on the half shell are very easy to do, and all they need is a sprinkling of Tabasco sauce, lemon or lime juice or soy sauce and perhaps a little very finely chopped fresh ginger to make a truly magnificent dish. Lobster on the Half Shell with Basil and Tomatoes (page 94) makes a wonderfully fragrant, luxurious dish that is absolute simplicity to prepare.

Placing the fish on greaseproof paper slows down the rate of cooking, as it shields the fish from direct contact with the steam; a wrapping of lettuce, spinach or vine leaves slows the cooking slightly as well as adding flavour to the flesh, whilst wrapping it in foil has an even greater effect. The rate of cooking is also slowed down if the fish is placed on a bed of vegetables or covered by vegetables. However, this method also keeps the heat in once the fish is removed from the steam so cooking times need to be slightly shorter to prevent the flesh becoming overcooked.

The variations in cooking times for the same-sized pieces of different types of fish are caused by the differences in the texture and structure of the flesh. Although salmon and tuna have dense, comparatively coarse-textured flesh the cooking times I have given are short because they are delicious when eaten 'rare'. But the fish must be very fresh.

Pieces of fish with the skin on should be cooked skin-side down and will take longer than skinned fish; bone in fish will also slow down the cooking.

FISH	WEIGHT	STEAMING TIME
Cod, boneless cutlet	115 g / 4 oz	3 mins
Cod steak	225 g / 8 oz	11–12 mins
Grey mullet	575 g / 1¼ lb	17–20 mins
Haddock fillet, skinned	150 g / 5 oz	1½ mins a side
Halibut fillet	150 g / 5 oz	2–2½ mins a side
Lobster, halved, in the shell	450–700 g / 1–1½ lb	8–10 mins
Monkfish, steak	175–200 g / 6–7 oz	6–6½ mins a side
cubes		2 mins
filleted tail	700 g / 1½ lb	18–20 mins
Mussels		2–3 mins
Plaice fillet	150 g / 5 oz	4–5 mins
Prawns	large	2 mins
Red mullet	small fillet	2 mins
Salmon, fillet	115–150 g / 4–5 oz	2–4 mins
steak	175 g / 6 oz	8–10 mins
Salmon trout, pieces	50 g / 2 oz	2 mins
fillet	150 g / 5 oz	3 mins
Sardines		4–5 mins
Scallop, on the half shell		2 mins
Sea bass, fillet	175 g / 6 oz	2–3 mins a side
whole fish	1 kg / 2 lb 2 oz	10–12 mins
Sole fillet	175 g / 6 oz	5 mins
Trout		4 mins a side
Tuna steaks	175 g / 6 oz	2–3 mins a side
Turbot steak	175 g / 6 oz	3 mins a side
medallions	175 g / 6 oz	3 mins a side

COD WITH GINGER AND SPRING ONIONS

SERVES 4

---

100 g/3½ oz SPRING ONIONS

PIECE OF PEELED FRESH ROOT GINGER, ABOUT
2.5 cm/1 in SQUARE

1 CLOVE OF GARLIC, CRUSHED

1 LIME OR SMALL LEMON

4 BONELESS COD CUTLETS, ABOUT 115 g/4 oz EACH,
1.25–2 cm/½–¾ in THICK

425 ml/¾ PINT FISH STOCK, SEE PAGE 20

150 g/5 oz FROMAGE BLANC

SALT AND FRESHLY GROUND BLACK PEPPER

Reserve 65 g/2½ oz of the spring onions. Chop the remaining spring onions, then pound to a smooth paste in a mortar with the ginger, garlic, 1 teaspoon finely grated lime or lemon rind and 1 teaspoon lime or lemon juice. Spread this paste over the cod, cover and leave in a cool place for about an hour.

Meanwhile, pare the remaining rind from the lime or lemon in long strips, blanch it in boiling water for 3 minutes, refresh, drain, cut into fine strips and reserve.

Carefully scrape the paste from the cod and add it to the fish stock then steam the fish over the stock for about 2 minutes. Remove from the heat and keep warm.

Boil the stock until reduced to 50 ml/2 fl oz.

While you are waiting, slice the reserved spring onions finely on the diagonal.

Reduce the heat beneath the stock to very low then gradually whisk in the fromage blanc. Stir in the spring onions and reserved lime or lemon strips. Season with salt and pepper, adding a little lime or lemon juice, if necessary. Serve the fish with the sauce poured over.

VARIATION

This fromage blanc marinade gives a tangy creaminess to the outside of the cod.

Pound a 2.5 cm / 1 in piece of peeled root ginger, 25 g / 1 oz chopped spring onions, 1 crushed clove of garlic, 1 teaspoon finely grated lime or lemon rind with 115 g / 4 oz fromage blanc. Spread over the cod and leave, covered, for about an hour. Steam the cod over the stock for about 2–2½ minutes. Meanwhile, very gently warm any remaining marinade, stirring. Add a little lime or lemon juice and serve warm with the fish.

COD STEAKS WITH DRIED ORANGE PEEL

SERVES 4

Although the delicate flavour of the fish is enhanced by the sauce, if you are diet conscious the sauce can be omitted. Dried orange or tangerine peel is available from Chinese and specialist food shops.

———

6 TABLESPOONS CHOPPED DRIED TANGERINE OR ORANGE PEEL

4 COD STEAKS, ABOUT 225 g / 8 oz EACH

450 ml / 16 fl oz FISH STOCK (OPTIONAL), SEE PAGE 20

75 g / 3 oz UNSALTED BUTTER, DICED

APPROX 1 TABLESPOON CASTER SUGAR

———

Make 4 beds out of the tangerine or orange peel to fit beneath the cod steaks on the bottom of a steaming basket, colander or rack, and place a cod steak on each bed. Steam over the stock, or seasoned water, for 11–12 minutes.

Remove the basket, colander or rack from the pan, carefully lift the fish, take out the tangerine or orange peel and add it to the steaming liquid. Cover the fish and keep warm.

Boil the steaming liquid until reduced to 150 ml/¼ pint. Pass through a strainer to remove the peel, then return to a low heat. Whisk in the butter, making sure each piece is incorporated before adding the next. Stir in the sugar and boil until reduced to 75 ml/3 fl oz. Serve the cod steaks with the sauce poured over.

HADDOCK WITH SPECIAL PARSLEY SAUCE

SERVES 4

The aniseed taste of pastis gives this sauce an interesting flavour. It is powerful, so add it carefully, a few drops at a time, until the taste is to your liking.

---

1 SHALLOT, FINELY CHOPPED

2 SPRIGS OF PARSLEY

1 SMALL SPRIG OF TARRAGON

225 ml/8 fl oz FISH STOCK, SEE PAGE 20

4 PIECES OF FILLETED HADDOCK, ABOUT 150 g/5 oz EACH, SKINNED

175 ml/6 fl oz DOUBLE CREAM OR FROMAGE BLANC

2 TABLESPOONS FINELY CHOPPED PARSLEY

1 TEASPOON FINELY CHOPPED TARRAGON

SALT AND FRESHLY GROUND BLACK PEPPER

1 TEASPOON PASTIS

LEMON JUICE

SPRIGS OF PARSLEY, FOR GARNISH

Add the shallot and herb sprigs to the stock then steam the haddock over the stock for 1½ minutes each side. Remove from the heat and keep warm.

Remove the herbs from the pan and boil the stock until reduced to 25 ml/1 fl oz. Purée with the cream, or fromage blanc, and chopped herbs. If cream has been used, boil until slightly thickened; if fromage blanc has been used, reheat gently, stirring, and do not allow to boil.

Season and flavour with a few drops of pastis, and a little lemon juice, if necessary.

Serve the fish with the sauce poured around and garnished with sprigs of parsley.

MONKFISH WITH LIME AND HERBS

SERVES 4

The character of this dish depends on the fresh lime juice, but if unavailable, use the juice of a small lemon – this changes the flavour slightly but with equally good results.

---

1 MONKFISH TAIL, WITHOUT THE VERY NARROW PART AT THE END, WEIGHING ABOUT 1 kg/2 lb 2 oz

A BOUQUET GARNI

JUICE OF 1 LIME

7 g/¼ oz (APPROX 5 TABLESPOONS) CHOPPED MIXED HERBS, E.G. BASIL, MARJORAM OR OREGANO, PARSLEY, THYME, DILL, FENNEL, MINT OR A LITTLE ROSEMARY

FRESHLY GROUND BLACK PEPPER

50 g/2 oz SHALLOTS, FINELY CHOPPED

4 TABLESPOONS DRY WHITE VERMOUTH (OPTIONAL)

JUICE OF ½ A LEMON

15 g/½ oz UNSALTED BUTTER, DICED, OR 25 g/1 oz FROMAGE BLANC (BOTH OPTIONAL)

SMALL SPRIGS OF HERBS, FOR GARNISH

Remove all traces of skin from the monkfish. Take out the central bone, then place the trimmings and bone in about 350 ml/12 fl oz water, seasoned with a fresh bouquet garni. Simmer for about 20 minutes, cover and leave to stand until required. Strain before using.

Sprinkle a little lime juice over the monkfish and press about a quarter of the herbs into the cut flesh. Tie the tail into a neat shape with string. Sprinkle the remaining lime juice and herbs over the fish and season lightly with black pepper. Put the fish in a non-metallic dish, cover and leave in a cool place for about an hour.

In a steamer or large saucepan, simmer the shallots in the vermouth, if used, until the liquid has reduced to 1 tablespoon, then stir in the lemon juice and strained stock. If vermouth is not used, add the shallots and lemon juice to the strained stock.

Lift the fish from the dish and pour any juices into the stock. Lay the fish in a steaming basket or colander and steam over this liquid for 18–20 minutes. Remove the basket or colander from the pan and keep the fish warm.

Boil the steaming liquor until reduced to 150 ml/¼ pint. (Strain the liquor if you want a smooth sauce, but I prefer to leave the shallots in.) Over a low heat, gradually stir in the butter or fromage blanc, if used. Taste and adjust the seasoning.

Remove the string holding the tail, and cut the fish into thick slices. Serve with the sauce poured over and garnish with small sprigs of herbs.

MONKFISH 'OSSO-BUCCO'

SERVES 4

This dish is so-called because the pieces of monkfish resemble the cut of veal used for the traditional Italian dish of osso-bucco.

---

50 g/2 oz SHELLED YOUNG PEAS OR FROZEN PETITS POIS, THAWED

1 YOUNG CARROT, DICED

2 SLIM STICKS OF CELERY, FINELY CHOPPED

3 SPRING ONIONS, THINLY SLICED

2 TOMATOES, SKINNED AND SEEDS REMOVED, CHOPPED

2 TABLESPOONS FINELY SHREDDED BASIL

SALT AND FRESHLY GROUND WHITE PEPPER

4 MONKFISH STEAKS CUT ACROSS THE BONE, ABOUT 175–200 g/6–7 oz EACH

350 ml/12 fl oz FISH STOCK, SEE PAGE 20

2 TABLESPOONS CAPERS

175 ml/6 fl oz MEDIUM-BODIED DRY WHITE WINE

25 g/1 oz UNSALTED BUTTER, DICED

GRATED RIND OF 1 LEMON

2 TABLESPOONS FINELY CHOPPED PARSLEY

Mix together the peas, carrot, celery, spring onions, tomatoes and basil and season lightly. Place about a third of this mixture on the base of a steaming basket or large colander. Place the monkfish steaks quite close together on top and cover with the remaining vegetable mixture. Steam over the stock for about 14–16 minutes, depending on the size of the pieces of fish, until almost cooked at the bone. Remove the basket or colander from the pan. Scatter the capers over the top of the vegetables, replace the lid and keep warm.

In a separate pan boil the wine until almost completely evaporated.

Stir in the steaming stock and boil until reduced by half. Lower the heat and gradually swirl in the butter, making sure each piece is fully incorporated before adding the next. Taste and adjust the seasoning.

Serve the monkfish and vegetables with the sauce poured over, and sprinkle with the lemon rind and parsley.

MONKFISH QUENELLES

SERVES 4

Using fromage blanc instead of cream makes a much lighter quenelle and cooking over steam prevents the mixture from breaking up.

---

150 g/5 oz FILLETED MONKFISH, CHOPPED AND CHILLED

PINCH OF SALT

1 EGG WHITE

300 g/10 oz FROMAGE BLANC

200 ml/7 fl oz FISH STOCK, SEE PAGE 20

75 ml/3 fl oz MEDIUM-BODIED DRY WHITE WINE

25 g/1 oz FRESH ROOT GINGER, PEELED AND CUT INTO 2 cm/¾ in LONG FINE STRIPS, WITH THE PEEL RESERVED

FRESHLY GROUND WHITE PEPPER

SMALL SPRIGS OF TARRAGON, FOR GARNISH

Purée the monkfish with the salt until smooth. Blend in the egg white. Stir in half of the fromage blanc and purée again. Cover and chill.

Lay a sheet of greaseproof paper in the bottom of a steaming basket or colander. Using a cold tablespoon, form the monkfish mousseline into small cigar shapes, placing each one on the greaseproof paper. Steam the quenelles over the stock and wine for 2 minutes. Remove from the heat and keep warm.

Add the ginger peelings to the steaming liquor and boil until reduced to about 50 ml/2 fl oz, or slightly syrupy. With a slotted spoon lift out the ginger peelings, take the stock off the heat and stir in the remaining fromage blanc and the strips of ginger. Reheat very gently over a low heat, stirring with a wooden spoon. Taste and adjust the seasoning.

Pour the sauce on to 4 warmed plates and gently place the quenelles on top. Garnish with small sprigs of tarragon.

RED MULLET WRAPPED IN VINE LEAVES

SERVES 4

3 TABLESPOONS MEDIUM-BODIED DRY WHITE WINE

1 TABLESPOON OLIVE OIL

3 TABLESPOONS LEMON JUICE

1 TABLESPOON EACH CHOPPED PARSLEY, FENNEL
AND THYME

FRESHLY GROUND BLACK PEPPER

4 RED MULLET, 175–225 g/6–8 oz EACH, CLEANED,
HEADS AND TAILS LEFT ON

APPROX 12 LARGE VINE LEAVES, LIGHTLY OILED
LEMON SLICES AND SPRIGS OF FENNEL,
FOR GARNISH

Beat together the wine, oil, lemon juice, herbs and black pepper then spread over both sides of the fish. Lay the fish in a shallow, non-metallic dish and leave in a cool place for 2 hours.

Remove the fish from the marinade, wrap each one in lightly oiled vine leaves, and steam, seam-side down, for about 8–10 minutes, depending on the size of the fish.

Serve with the remaining marinade spooned over. Garnish with lemon slices and sprigs of fennel.

RED MULLET WITH CORIANDER SEED DRESSING

SERVES 2

This dish is also very good served as a light summer first course for four.

2 MEDIUM-SIZED RED MULLET
LEMON JUICE
10 SPRIGS OF THYME
150 ml/¼ PINT EXTRA VIRGIN OLIVE OIL
25 g/1 oz CORIANDER SEEDS, CRACKED
2 CLOVES OF GARLIC, PEELED BUT LEFT WHOLE
4 FIRM TOMATOES, SKINNED AND SEEDS
REMOVED, DICED
SALT AND FRESHLY GROUND BLACK PEPPER
FISH STOCK FOR STEAMING (OPTIONAL),
SEE PAGE 20
SMALL HEAD OF FRISÉE LETTUCE

Fillet the fish and remove the scales. Squeeze lemon juice over the skin and place a sprig of thyme on each fillet.

Gently heat the olive oil, coriander seeds, garlic and 2 sprigs of thyme. Leave to cool, then remove the garlic and thyme. Add the tomatoes. Season lightly and set aside.

Place each fillet on a sprig of thyme and lay in a steaming basket or colander. Steam over the fish stock, or seasoned water, for about 1½–2 minutes. Turn the fillets over; make sure there is a sprig of thyme on top and beneath each fillet. Steam for a further 1½–2 minutes, or until the flesh feels firm when gently pressed.

Make a bed of lettuce on 4 plates and lay the fish, skin side up, on top. Spoon a little of the dressing over each fillet.

PINK AND WHITE
PARCELS

SERVES 4

8 LARGE CHARD OR SPINACH LEAVES, STALKS
REMOVED, BLANCHED BRIEFLY, REFRESHED AND
DRAINED

1 TABLESPOON LEMON JUICE

225 g/8 oz SKINNED SALMON FILLET, CUT INTO
4 PIECES

FRESHLY GROUND BLACK PEPPER

4 SPRIGS OF DILL

450 g/1 lb SKINNED TURBOT FILLET, CUT INTO
8 PIECES

100 ml/3½ fl oz MEDIUM-BODIED DRY WHITE WINE

STRIP OF LEMON PEEL

300 ml/½ PINT FISH STOCK, SEE PAGE 20

100 ml/3½ fl oz DOUBLE CREAM OR FROMAGE BLANC
OR GREEK YOGHURT

TOMATO PURÉE

8 LONG STRIPS OF RED PEPPER, SKINNED AND BLANCHED (OPTIONAL)

Spread out the chard or spinach leaves to dry on absorbent kitchen paper. Sprinkle a little lemon juice on each piece of salmon. Season lightly with black pepper, then place a sprig of dill on each. Sandwich each piece of salmon between 2 pieces of turbot, then enclose securely in 2 chard or spinach leaves and tie with string.

Add the wine and lemon peel to the stock. Place the parcels in a steaming basket or colander and steam over the stock for 5 minutes. Remove the basket or colander from the pan and keep the fish warm.

Boil the steaming liquor until reduced to 75 ml / 3 fl oz. Remove the lemon peel. If using cream, stir in and boil until slightly thickened. If using fromage blanc or Greek yoghurt, reduce the heat to very low and then stir in. Add just enough tomato purée to give a delicate pink colour. Season with black pepper to taste and add a little lemon juice, if necessary.

Remove the string from the fish parcels. To garnish, lay strips of blanched, skinned red pepper over the parcels to resemble the string. Pour the sauce on to 4 warmed plates and place the parcels on top. If you are not using red pepper, make a cut about three-quarters of the way through each parcel and open it out slightly to show the colours inside.

SALMON WITH MINT VINAIGRETTE

SERVES 4

If they are available, fresh tuna steaks can be used in this recipe.

---

4 SALMON STEAKS, 150–175 g/5–6 oz EACH

FRESHLY GROUND WHITE PEPPER

2 TABLESPOONS CHOPPED MINT

115 ml/4 fl oz EXTRA VIRGIN OLIVE OIL

1 TABLESPOON LIME JUICE

1 TABLESPOON WHITE WINE VINEGAR

1 TABLESPOON FINELY CHOPPED PARSLEY

6 TOMATOES, SKINNED AND SEEDS REMOVED, DICED

2 CLOVES OF GARLIC, BLANCHED AND CUT INTO FINE STRIPS

SALT AND FRESHLY GROUND BLACK PEPPER

FISH STOCK FOR STEAMING (OPTIONAL), SEE PAGE 20

SMALL SPRIGS OF MINT, FOR GARNISH

Sprinkle the salmon steaks with white pepper, then put in a shallow, non-metallic dish. Mix together 1 tablespoon mint and 2 tablespoons oil, spoon over the fish and leave to marinate for 3 hours, turning the fish occasionally.

Combine the remaining ingredients (except the fish stock, if used, and the garnish) for the vinaigrette and set aside.

Lift the salmon from the marinade, allowing the excess to drain off. Lay the salmon in a steaming basket or colander and steam over the fish stock, or seasoned water, for 3–4 minutes each side.

Stir the vinaigrette and spoon on to 4 plates, place the fish on top and garnish with sprigs of mint.

SALMON WITH CUCUMBER

SERVES 4

---

1 MEDIUM-SIZED CUCUMBER, PEELED AND SEEDS
REMOVED, CHOPPED

4 SALMON STEAKS, ABOUT 175 g/6 oz EACH

SALT AND FRESHLY GROUND WHITE PEPPER

115 ml/4 fl oz DRY WHITE VERMOUTH

2 TABLESPOONS CHOPPED CHIVES

75 ml/3 fl oz STRAINED GREEK YOGHURT, OR OTHER
THICK YOGHURT

SHORT, FINE STRIPS OF LEMON PEEL AND
CUCUMBER PEEL, FOR GARNISH

In a steaming basket or colander, steam the cucumber for about 2 minutes, until beginning to soften, then purée roughly in a food processor or blender.

Season the salmon lightly and place on a large heatproof plate or in a shallow dish. Spoon the vermouth over, cover with another large plate or foil and place in a steaming basket or on a rack. Steam for about 15–17 minutes, so the fish is very lightly cooked, turning it over half-way through.

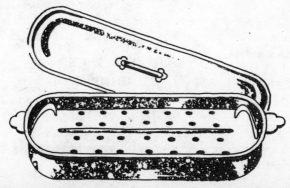

Pour off the cooking juices and boil until reduced to 1 tablespoon. Keep the salmon warm.

Add the reduced cooking juices, chives and yoghurt to the puréed cucumber and purée briefly so the sauce has a little texture. Reheat the sauce gently, stirring with a wooden spoon – do not allow it to boil. Taste and adjust the seasoning. Divide between 4 warmed plates. Place the salmon on top, and garnish with the strips of lemon and cucumber peels.

SPECIAL FISH PUDDING
SERVES 4

A steam pudding that is both tasty and light. To make it extra special, serve with the Herb Hollandaise Sauce on page 28.

———

200 g/7 oz SELF-RAISING FLOUR
PINCH OF SALT
100 g/3½ oz SUET
FINELY GRATED RIND OF 2 LEMONS
2 TABLESPOONS FINELY CHOPPED THYME
SALT AND FRESHLY GROUND BLACK PEPPER
A LITTLE MILK

———

FILLING
25 g/1 oz BUTTER, DICED
1 SHALLOT, CHOPPED
100 g/3½ oz WILD MUSHROOMS OR OYSTER
MUSHROOMS, CHOPPED
1 LARGE BAY LEAF, BROKEN
1 TABLESPOON FINELY CHOPPED PARSLEY
150 ml/¼ PINT MILK

450 g / 1 lb HADDOCK FILLET, SKINNED AND CHOPPED
1 CAN SMOKED OYSTERS, DRAINED
RIND AND JUICE OF 1 LARGE LEMON

Sift together the flour and salt, then stir in the suet, lemon rind, thyme and a little salt and pepper. Make a well in the centre and gradually pour in sufficient milk to form a smooth, pliable, soft, but not sticky, dough.

Transfer to a lightly floured surface, knead briefly, then cut off a third of the dough. Roll the larger piece of dough to a circle about 7.5 cm / 3 in wider than the top of a 1 litre / 2 pint pudding basin, and use to line the lightly buttered basin.

For the filling, melt the butter in a pan, add the shallot and mushrooms and cook for 3–4 minutes, stirring occasionally. Add the bay leaf, parsley and milk and simmer for 2–3 minutes. Remove from the heat, discard the bay leaf, and add the haddock, oysters, lemon juice and rind. Season and transfer to the pastry-lined basin.

Roll out the reserved piece of dough to make a lid for the pudding. Dampen the edge of the lining dough then put on the lid, lightly pressing the edges together to seal. Cover the top of the basin with a piece of greaseproof paper that has been pleated across the centre. Cover with foil, place in a steaming basket or colander and steam for 1½–2 hours.

FISH SOUFFLÉ PUDDING

SERVES 4

The unglamorous title hardly does justice to what is actually a rather pleasant, light fish dish, but it describes the recipe exactly. As a slight variation, include some shellfish such as crabmeat, shrimps or diced prawns in the blend of fish, and flavour with chopped herbs.

---

400 g/14 oz COOKED FISH, EITHER ONE TYPE OR A MIXTURE WHICH CAN INCLUDE HADDOCK, COD, A LITTLE MONKFISH OR SALMON

100 g/3½ oz BREAD, CRUSTS REMOVED, SOAKED IN MILK THEN SQUEEZED

3 EGGS, SEPARATED

SALT AND FRESHLY GROUND BLACK PEPPER

LEMON JUICE

ANCHOVY ESSENCE

Pound the fish and bread in a mortar, transfer to a bowl and gradually beat in the egg yolks. In a separate bowl whisk the egg whites until stiff, but not dry. Fold into the fish mixture and season well, adding lemon juice and anchovy essence to boost the flavour, if necessary.

Transfer to a buttered 1 litre/2 pint soufflé dish or charlotte mould, cover loosely with greaseproof paper, place in a steaming basket or colander, cover with a dome of foil and steam for 40 minutes, until risen and lightly set in the centre. Serve immediately.

ROLLED FILLETS OF SOLE AND SMOKED SALMON

SERVES 4

You can vary this recipe by leaving out the smoked salmon and, instead, rolling up chopped prawns or thinly spread herb-flavoured soft cheese inside.

---

4 THIN SLICES OF SMOKED SALMON
4 FILLETS OF SOLE, ABOUT 100–115 g/3½–4 oz EACH
FRESHLY GROUND BLACK PEPPER
3 TABLESPOONS LEMON JUICE
8 LETTUCE LEAVES
225 ml/8 fl oz FISH STOCK, SEE PAGE 20
225 ml/8 fl oz MEDIUM-BODIED DRY WHITE WINE
115 g/4 oz UNSALTED BUTTER, DICED
SALT AND FRESHLY GROUND WHITE PEPPER
BASIL LEAVES AND TOMATO FLESH, DICED,
FOR GARNISH

Lay the slices of salmon on the sole and sprinkle with black pepper and a little of the lemon juice. Steam the lettuce leaves for about a minute to soften, then lay them out in pairs, overlapping slightly. Place the fish slices on the lettuce leaves and roll up like a Swiss roll. Transfer to a basket, rack or colander, keeping the seam underneath, and steam over the stock, wine and remaining lemon juice for 3–4 minutes. Remove from the heat and keep warm.

Boil the steaming liquid until reduced to 50 ml/2 fl oz. Lower the heat and gradually stir in the butter, making sure each piece is incorporated before adding the next. Season with salt and white pepper and add a little more lemon juice, if necessary.

Cut the fish rolls into slices, pour the sauce on to 4 warmed plates and serve the fish slices on top. Garnish with basil leaves and tomato.

FILLETS OF SOLE WITH FENNEL-SCENTED LEMON SAUCE

SERVES 4

It will probably be necessary to cook the sole in batches, so make sure the first ones steamed are only very lightly cooked. Serve with a colourful, crisp vegetable.

---

4 FILLETS OF SOLE, ABOUT 175 g/6 oz EACH
1 SHALLOT, CHOPPED
1 YOUNG CARROT, QUARTERED
4 GOOD-SIZED SPRIGS OF FENNEL
2 EGG YOLKS
1 TABLESPOON LEMON JUICE
SCANT ½ TEASPOON HERB MUSTARD
50 g/2 oz MEDIUM-FAT CURD CHEESE
200 ml/7 fl oz STRAINED GREEK YOGHURT
SALT AND FRESHLY GROUND BLACK PEPPER (OPTIONAL)
SMALL SPRIGS OF FENNEL, FOR GARNISH

Steam the sole in a single layer, skin-side down and flat, over 300 ml/½ pint water flavoured with the shallot, carrot and fennel for about 3 minutes, until very lightly cooked. Remove from the heat and keep warm.

To make the sauce, boil the steaming liquid until reduced to 2 tablespoons, removing the shallot and carrot when the reduction is almost complete. Strain the liquid into a small, preferably nonstick, saucepan, then stir in the egg yolks, lemon juice, mustard, curd cheese and yoghurt. Cook over a very low heat, stirring constantly, until the sauce thickens. Taste and adjust the seasoning, if necessary.

Pour the sauce on to 4 warmed plates, arrange the fish on top and garnish with several small sprigs of fennel.

SOLE WITH LETTUCE FILLING

SERVES 4

---

1 TABLESPOON MEDIUM-BODIED DRY WHITE WINE
1 TABLESPOON FINELY CHOPPED WHITE
PART OF LEEK
75 g/3 oz ICEBERG LETTUCE, SHREDDED
75 g/3 oz RICOTTA CHEESE, SIEVED
SALT AND FRESHLY GROUND WHITE PEPPER
4 FILLETS OF SOLE
SQUEEZE OF LEMON JUICE
1 EGG WHITE

Heat the wine in a small saucepan, add the leek, cover and cook for 2–3 minutes, shaking the pan occasionally. Add the lettuce, cover and cook, until the lettuce has 'fallen'. Uncover the pan and increase the heat to drive off excess moisture, if necessary. Purée the mixture with the ricotta cheese. Season with salt and pepper.

Season the fillets lightly and squeeze over a little lemon juice.

Whisk the egg white until stiff, but not dry, then fold into the lettuce mixture. Place some of this mixture on to half of each fish fillet, then fold the other half lightly over the filling. Steam for about 10–12 minutes until the filling is just set. Leave for a minute or so then carefully transfer to warmed plates, using a fish slice.

TROUT WITH BAY LEAVES

SERVES 4

---

8 BAY LEAVES

4 FRESH TROUT, ABOUT 225 g/8 oz EACH, CLEANED

2 TABLESPOONS VIRGIN OLIVE OIL

115 ml/4 fl oz DRY WHITE VERMOUTH

FISH STOCK FOR STEAMING (OPTIONAL),
SEE PAGE 20

JUICE OF 1 LARGE ORANGE

JUICE OF 1 LEMON

25 g/1 oz UNSALTED BUTTER, DICED

SALT AND FRESHLY GROUND BLACK PEPPER

Cut 4 of the bay leaves into 8 pieces each. With the point of a small sharp knife, make 4 small slits in the skin on each side of the fish, taking care not to pierce the flesh. Carefully insert a piece of bay leaf into each slit and place a whole bay leaf inside each fish.

Mix together the olive oil and half of the vermouth, then gently rub into the skin of each fish and leave in a cool place for about 2 hours. Steam over the fish stock, or seasoned water, for 4 minutes each side. Remove from the heat and keep warm.

In a separate pan, boil the remaining vermouth until almost completely evaporated, then stir in the orange and lemon juices. Boil for a minute or two, lower the heat and gradually swirl in the butter, making sure each piece is incorporated before adding the next. Season lightly and spoon over the fish to serve.

TROUT WITH CUCUMBER AND MINT

SERVES 4

This is a simple, light, fresh-tasting dish with a slightly crunchy texture. It tastes just as good flavoured with dill instead of mint.

---

4 TROUT, ABOUT 225 g/8 oz EACH, HEADS AND TAILS REMOVED

1 TABLESPOON FINELY CHOPPED MINT

200 g/7 oz CUCUMBER, PEELED AND SEEDS REMOVED, FINELY DICED

4 TABLESPOONS FROMAGE BLANC

2 TABLESPOONS EGG WHITE

SALT AND FRESHLY GROUND BLACK PEPPER

MINT LEAVES, FOR GARNISH (OPTIONAL)

GENTLY WARMED SEASONED FROMAGE BLANC OR SOURED CREAM, TO SERVE (OPTIONAL)

First, cut away the fins from the fish. Place each trout on the work surface with the backbone uppermost and the sides laid outwards. Using your thumbs, gently press along the backbone to loosen it. Turn the fish over and ease the backbone and side bones away from the flesh.

Mix together the mint, cucumber, fromage blanc, egg white, salt and pepper. Lightly season inside the fish, then divide the filling equally among them. Close securely with wooden cocktail sticks. Wrap each trout in a parcel of lightly seasoned foil and steam for about 17 minutes.

Either leave the trout in their parcels or transfer them to warmed plates. Garnish with mint leaves, and serve with gently warmed and seasoned fromage blanc or soured cream, if you wish.

MEDALLIONS OF TURBOT WITH BASIL

SERVES 4

---

25 ml/1 fl oz DRY WHITE VERMOUTH
300 ml/½ PINT FISH STOCK, SEE PAGE 20
16 BASIL LEAVES
4 MEDALLIONS OF TURBOT, ABOUT 175 g/6 oz EACH
150 g/5 oz FROMAGE BLANC
SALT AND FRESHLY GROUND WHITE PEPPER
(OPTIONAL)

Add the vermouth to the stock. Place a basil leaf on top of each medallion, then steam the turbot over the stock and vermouth for about 6 minutes. Remove from the heat and keep warm.

Boil the steaming liquor until reduced to 50 ml/2 fl oz. Turn down the heat to very low and gradually whisk in the fromage blanc. Shred the remaining basil leaves and add to the sauce. Taste and season, if necessary.

Serve the turbot with the sauce poured around.

SKATE ON A PLATE

SERVES 4

1.2 kg/2½ lb SKATE WINGS, IN 4 PIECES
SALT AND FRESHLY GROUND BLACK PEPPER
2 TABLESPOONS LEMON JUICE
3 TABLESPOONS EXTRA VIRGIN OLIVE OIL
2 TABLESPOONS FINELY CHOPPED PARSLEY
3 TABLESPOONS CHOPPED CAPERS
SLICES OF LEMON AND SPRIGS OF PARSLEY,
FOR GARNISH

Lay the skate in a single layer on a heatproof plate. Season with salt and pepper. Spoon over the lemon juice and olive oil and sprinkle with the parsley and capers. Cover and steam for 10 minutes.

Serve the fish with the juices poured over and garnish with slices of lemon and sprigs of parsley.

HERB-COATED
GOUJONS
SERVES 4

I usually use halibut for this recipe but other white fish, such as cod, plaice, brill or lemon sole, could be used instead. If you are using seasoned water instead of fish stock, use reduced wine instead of stock to make the sauce. Serve the fish with small side salads of curly endive and shredded young chicory leaves, tossed with a light walnut oil dressing.

---

575 g / 1¼ lb SKINNED AND BONED HALIBUT CUTLETS,
OR FILLETS
1 SHALLOT, FINELY CHOPPED
1 TABLESPOON FINELY CHOPPED CHIVES
1 TABLESPOON FINELY CHOPPED TARRAGON
1½ TEASPOONS FINELY CHOPPED PARSLEY
300 ml / ½ PINT FISH STOCK (OPTIONAL), SEE PAGE 20
1 TABLESPOON ORANGE JUICE
1½ TEASPOONS LEMON JUICE
1½ TEASPOONS FINELY GRATED ORANGE RIND
1 TABLESPOON FINELY GRATED LEMON RIND
3 TABLESPOONS EXTRA VIRGIN OLIVE OIL
1½ TEASPOONS WALNUT OR PEANUT OIL
APPROX 1 TABLESPOON CHOPPED LARGE CAPERS
FOR GARNISH

Cut the halibut flesh into strips about 1.25–2 × 7.5 cm / ½–¾ × 3 in.

Mix together the shallot, chives, tarragon and parsley, and roll the strips of halibut in this mixture to coat. Arrange in a single layer and steam over the stock for about 1½–2 minutes.

Meanwhile, in a separate bowl, mix together the fruit juices, rinds and oils.

Remove the fish from the heat and keep warm. Boil 50 ml/2 fl oz of the stock until reduced to 2 tablespoons. Meanwhile, carefully transfer the fish to a shallow serving dish. Stir the reduced stock into the oil mixture well, then pour over the fish immediately. Leave for about 10 minutes. Sprinkle with the capers and serve.

BREAM WITH SAFFRON SAUCE
SERVES 4

Saffron is one of the most evocative smells, culinary or otherwise, and it imparts a rich, luxurious flavour to food that is steamed over a liquid containing it. As an alternative to bream, other prime quality fish, such as sole, scallops or sea bass, can be given the same treatment. The butter gives a final sheen to the sauce but if you are being really careful about your diet, leave it out.

PACKET OF SAFFRON THREADS
175 ml/6 fl oz MEDIUM-BODIED DRY WHITE WINE
225 ml/8 fl oz FISH STOCK, SEE PAGE 20
4 FILLETS OF SEA BREAM, ABOUT 175 g/6 oz EACH
115 g/4 oz FROMAGE BLANC
20 g/¾ oz UNSALTED BUTTER, DICED AND SOFTENED
(OPTIONAL)
SALT AND FRESHLY GROUND WHITE PEPPER
LEMON JUICE
SMALL SPRIGS OF CHERVIL, FOR GARNISH

Steep the saffron in a little warmed wine for 5 minutes, then pour into a steamer or large pan containing the remaining wine and stock.

Steam the bream, in a single layer, over this liquid for about 3–3½ minutes each side. Remove from the heat and keep warm.

To make the sauce, boil the steaming liquid until reduced to 115 ml/4 fl oz. Stir in the fromage blanc and heat very gently – do not allow it to boil. At the same time, gradually swirl in the butter, if used, making sure each piece is fully incorporated before adding the next. Season with salt and pepper and add a little lemon juice, if necessary.

To serve, pour the sauce on to 4 warmed plates, lay the bream on top and garnish with sprigs of chervil.

SEA BASS IN GINGER VINAIGRETTE

SERVES 4

I have also used this recipe to great effect when cooking salmon and fresh tuna.

———————

1.25 cm/½ in PIECE FRESH ROOT GINGER, PEELED AND FINELY CHOPPED

1 SHALLOT, FINELY CHOPPED

25 ml/1 fl oz RICE WINE VINEGAR

115 ml/4 fl oz VIRGIN OLIVE OIL

JUICE OF 1 LIME

1 TABLESPOON SOY SAUCE

1 TABLESPOON SESAME OIL

SALT AND FRESHLY GROUND BLACK PEPPER

4 SEA BASS FILLETS, ABOUT 175 g/6 oz EACH

FISH STOCK FOR STEAMING (OPTIONAL), SEE PAGE 20

½ BUNCH FRESH CORIANDER OR FLAT-LEAVED PARSLEY, ROUGHLY CHOPPED

1 TABLESPOON TOASTED SESAME SEEDS

LEAVES OF CORIANDER OR FLAT-LEAVED PARSLEY, FOR GARNISH

———————

Mix together the ginger, shallot, vinegar, olive oil, lime juice and soy sauce. Whisk in the sesame oil and season with salt and pepper.

Lay the fish in a shallow dish, spoon over 4 tablespoons of the dressing and leave to marinate for 2 hours, turning the fish occasionally.

Lift the fish from the marinade, allowing the excess to drain off, then steam over the fish stock, or seasoned water, for about 1½–2 minutes each side.

Stir the coriander or parsley into the remaining dressing. To serve, pour the dressing on to 4 plates, place the fish on top and sprinkle with the sesame seeds. Garnish with coriander or parsley leaves.

PANACHE OF MIXED FISH

SERVES 4

The fish in this recipe can be varied depending on availability, but try to use varied textures and colours and include a shellfish.

---

115 g/4 oz SKINNED SALMON FILLET

½ TEASPOON EGG WHITE

SALT AND FRESHLY GROUND BLACK PEPPER

250 ml/8½ fl oz DOUBLE CREAM; 150 ml/4½ fl oz OF IT CHILLED

SMALL PINCH OF CAYENNE PEPPER

PINCH OF SAFFRON

200 ml/7 fl oz FISH STOCK, SEE PAGE 20

115 ml/4 fl oz MEDIUM-BODIED DRY WHITE WINE

1½ TEASPOONS LEMON JUICE

4 TYPES OF FISH E.G. FOUR 50 g/2 oz PIECES OF TURBOT FILLET, FOUR 50 g/2 oz PIECES OF SEA BASS FILLETS, FOUR 75 g/3 oz JOHN DORY FILLETS,

**4 SHELLED SCALLOPS, BODIES AND CORALS
SEPARATED
SPRIGS OF CHERVIL, FOR GARNISH**

Beat the salmon with the egg white and salt, then rub through a sieve into a bowl placed on ice. Gradually work in the chilled cream, keeping the mixture as cool as possible. Add the cayenne pepper. Pipe the mixture into 4 small metal tins, pushing it well into the sides.

In a steamer or large pan, infuse the saffron in a little of the stock for 5 minutes, then add the remaining stock, wine and lemon juice. Arrange the tins and the remaining fish over the liquid, allowing about 4–5 minutes for the moulds, until they are just set, and 2–3 minutes for the fish, depending on the type. Take care not to let them overcook. Remove the fish and tins from the heat. Leave the mousses to stand for a few minutes and keep the other fish warm.

Boil the liquid until reduced to 50 ml/2 fl oz. Lower the heat and stir in the remaining cream. Simmer for 2 minutes, taste and adjust the seasoning and add more lemon juice, if necessary.

Turn out the mousses, pour the sauce around and place the fish on top. Garnish with sprigs of chervil.

SEAFOOD POTS
SERVES 4

The best seafood pots are made from a mixture of about five types of
fish and shellfish. Choose from among John Dory, monkfish, red
mullet, sole, turbot, salmon, sea bass, Dublin Bay prawns, scallops
and mussels. If using sea bass, lay the fillets skin side up. The
wakame (a Japanese dried seaweed available from good supermarkets
and speciality shops) adds a real sea-fresh flavour and enhances the
wonderful aroma which wafts from the pots on opening. If, however,
wakame is unavailable, use shredded spinach and sorrel leaves.
Serve this dish with French bread to mop up the juices.

4 SHEETS OF WAKAME, SOAKED FOR 20 MINUTES
APPROX 450–575 g/1–1¼ lb FILLETED FISH AND
PREPARED SHELLFISH, CUT INTO 2.5 cm/1 in PIECES
25 g/1 oz EACH CARROT, COURGETTE, LEEK AND
CELERY, CUT INTO FINE STRIPS
150 ml/¼ PINT MEDIUM-BODIED DRY WHITE WINE
SEA SALT AND FRESHLY GROUND WHITE PEPPER
APPROX 40 g/1½ oz UNSALTED BUTTER (OPTIONAL)
4 SMALL SPRIGS OF FENNEL

Using 4 quite thick heatproof pots with lids, line the base of each with the wakame. Arrange all the fish on top – do not pack them too tightly. Toss together the vegetables, then divide between the pots. (In Japan this type of dish bears the name 'shiba' meaning brushwood as the strips of vegetables are arranged like wood laid on a fire.)

Sprinkle with the wine and season with sea salt and white pepper. Add a small knob of butter, if desired, then top with a sprig of fennel. Cover tightly with the lids (if they do not fit securely, first seal with foil or clingfilm), and steam for about 3–4 minutes, or until the fish are just cooked – the timing will depend on the types used, how tightly they are packed and the thickness of the pots.

SEAFOOD 'SAUSAGES'
SERVES 4

Good butchers should be able to supply sausage skins to order, but if
you cannot get them, form the mixture into 'sausages', encase in
clingfilm then remove the clingfilm before serving. Using this
method you may find it easier to serve the 'sausages' unsliced.

---

4 SCALLOPS

SALT AND FRESHLY GROUND WHITE PEPPER

4 DUBLIN BAY PRAWNS, REMOVED FROM
THEIR SHELLS

150 g/5 oz SKINNED MONKFISH FILLET, CUT INTO
SMALL CUBES

150 g/5 oz SKINNED SALMON FILLET, CUT INTO
SMALL CUBES

200 g/7 oz SKINNED SOLE FILLETS, CHILLED

SQUEEZE OF LEMON JUICE

1 EGG WHITE

225 g/8 oz FROMAGE BLANC, HALF OF IT CHILLED

SAUSAGE SKIN, APPROX 45 cm/18 in LONG, SOAKED

300 ml/½ PINT FISH STOCK, SEE PAGE 20

150 ml/¼ PINT MEDIUM-BODIED DRY WHITE WINE

2 SHALLOTS, QUARTERED

20 g/¾ oz CHOPPED CHIVES

Separate the corals from the bodies of the scallops. Cut the bodies and
corals into small cubes, then place them on a cloth to dry. Lightly
season all the fish with salt and pepper. Purée the sole with a squeeze
of lemon juice then add the egg white and a little salt and pepper. Mix
thoroughly until smooth, then gradually work in the chilled fromage
blanc. Add the scallops, prawns, monkfish and salmon. Cover and chill
for about half an hour.

By using an attachment on a food mixer, a piping bag fitted with a large, plain nozzle, or a small spoon, fill the sausage skin to make sausages about 2 cm/¾ in wide. Twist at approximately 10 cm/4 in intervals and tie both ends. Steam over the fish stock, wine and shallots for 3–4 minutes, turning the sausages over half-way through. Remove from the heat and keep warm.

Boil the steaming liquor and shallots until the liquor is reduced to 115 ml/4 fl oz. Remove the shallots, then purée the liquor and half of the chives. Purée again with the remaining fromage blanc. Add the rest of the chives and reheat gently, stirring – do not allow the sauce to boil. Taste and season, adding a little lemon juice if necessary.

Slice the sausages diagonally. Pour the sauce on to 4 warmed plates and serve the sausages on top.

BRILL AND BUTTERED SHRIMP PARCELS

SERVES 4

Chopped prawns can be used instead of shrimps and sole fillets can replace the brill.

---

75 g/3 oz UNSALTED BUTTER, DICED
1 TABLESPOON VERY FINELY CHOPPED SHALLOT
75 g/3 oz SHRIMPS, SHELLED AND COOKED
1 TABLESPOON LEMON JUICE
PINCH EACH OF FRESHLY GRATED NUTMEG AND
CAYENNE PEPPER
1 SMALL HARD WHITE CABBAGE
175 g/6 oz BRILL FILLET, SKINNED
SALT AND FRESHLY GROUND BLACK PEPPER

Melt the butter, add the shallot and heat gently. Remove from the heat and pour into a bowl containing the shrimps. Stir in the lemon juice, nutmeg and cayenne pepper, then leave to set.

On a piece of clingfilm, form the mixture into a roll about 4 cm/ 1½ in diameter. Roll up the clingfilm and chill well – half an hour or so in the freezer or top part of a refrigerator will do.

Carefully remove 4 leaves from the cabbage that will form natural 'cups'. Cut out the thickest part of the central stem, then blanch the leaves for one minute. Refresh under cold running water, drain and dry. Remove the central stems from the remaining cabbage leaves and chop the leaves finely. Blanch for 30 seconds. Refresh, drain and dry well.

Cut the brill into 4 pieces, season, then place individually in a cabbage leaf 'cup'. Place a quarter of the chopped cabbage on each piece of fish. Unwrap the buttered shrimp roll and cut off 4 slices, approximately 2 cm/¾ in thick. Arrange a slice on each pile of cabbage. Fold the cabbage leaves over to make parcels, then steam for 4 minutes, until the fish is just cooked and the buttered shrimps are just beginning to melt.

Serve on warmed plates with a little of the remaining shrimp butter to the side.

LOBSTER ON THE HALF SHELL WITH BASIL AND TOMATOES

SERVES 2–4

It is well worth buying lobsters that are alive. Freezing shrinks the flesh and tends to make it tough, spoiling its wonderful texture and flavour. But if you don't want to kill the lobster yourself, ask the fishmonger to do it for you and cook it as soon as possible.

4–5 TABLESPOONS FINELY SHREDDED BASIL

1 TEASPOON EXTRA VIRGIN OLIVE OIL

1 RIPE TOMATO, SKINNED AND SEEDS REMOVED, CHOPPED

FRESHLY GROUND BLACK PEPPER

2 LIVE LOBSTERS, PREFERABLY FEMALE, ABOUT 450–700 g / 1–1½ lb EACH

Pound together in a mortar the basil, oil and tomato, then season with black pepper to taste.

Kill the lobsters by plunging the point of a sharp, firm-bladed knife into the centre of the cross marked on the shell of the head. Then place the lobster on a board with the tail spread out flat and push the point of a chopping knife firmly into the cross. Hold the side of the lobster firmly and bring the knife down to where the tail meets the body and split it in two. Remove the gritty 'sac' behind the eyes, the gills and the intestinal vein in the meat that runs down the middle of the tail. Make a few diagonal slashes in the flesh of each half lobster. Spread the basil mixture over the flesh, then steam for about 8–10 minutes, until just cooked.

Serve hot or cold.

MUSSELS WITH HERBS AND WINE

SERVES 2

---

300 ml / ½ PINT MEDIUM-BODIED DRY WHITE WINE

3 BLACK AND 3 WHITE PEPPERCORNS,
LIGHTLY CRUSHED

2 TABLESPOONS CHOPPED PARSLEY,
STALKS RETAINED

SPRIG OF FENNEL

SEA SALT

900 g / 2 lb MUSSELS IN THEIR SHELLS, SCRUBBED,
BEARDS REMOVED

2 TABLESPOONS FINELY CHOPPED FENNEL

Pour the wine into a steamer or large pan, then add the peppercorns, parsley stalks, sprig of fennel and a little sea salt. Steam the mussels over this liquid for 2–3 minutes until they have opened. Discard any that remain closed.

Transfer the mussels to a large, warm tureen. Strain the cooking liquor and pour over. Sprinkle with chopped fennel and parsley.

WARM PRAWN SALAD WITH ORANGE CORIANDER DRESSING

SERVES 4

Jalapeno chillis are short, fat, green and hot. If you are unable to find any, substitute with another hot, fresh chilli.

Serve the prawns on four individual plates of salad which might include feuille de Chêne (red oak leaf lettuce), lollo rosso or quattro stagioni, all available from good supermarkets.

1 LARGE ORANGE

3 SPRIGS OF FRESH CORIANDER, LEAVES AND STEMS
FINELY CHOPPED

2 TABLESPOONS OLIVE OIL

1 TABLESPOON WHITE WINE VINEGAR

1 JALAPENO CHILLI, SEEDS REMOVED, FINELY
CHOPPED

SALT

16 LARGE PRAWNS, PEELED, DE-VEINED, BUT TAILS
LEFT ON

3 TABLESPOONS LEMON JUICE

4 SMALL SALADS, E.G. WATERCRESS, CUCUMBER,
SKINNED AND SEEDS REMOVED, CUT INTO STRIPS

Grate the orange rind. Working over a bowl to catch the juice and using a small, stainless-steel knife, pare away the white pith then cut between the membranes to remove the segments. Chop these and add to the juice, followed by the orange rind, coriander, oil, vinegar, chilli and salt. Set aside.

Curl the prawns into 'C' shapes and thread on to fine skewers, spacing them at least 2.5 cm / 1 in apart. Place in a non-metallic dish, pour the lemon juice over and leave for 10–15 minutes.

Steam the prawns for 2 minutes.

Arrange the prawns on the small salads with the orange coriander dressing poured over.

POULTRY AND GAME

This is a successful group of food, as not only does steaming produce moist, succulent and tasty chicken (even the most simple recipe, such as Country Chicken, page 117, transforms a frozen broiler into a meltingly juicy bird with a good flavour), poussins, spring chicken and farmed rabbit but also, and I'll admit slightly to my surprise, steaming works well with duck breasts and all game birds, including pigeon, in particular.

Steaming eliminates the need to lard or baste lean poultry and game with fat to keep it moist. And overcooking with its attendant drying out, hardening of the flesh and loss of flavour, which can happen with such ease when game and poultry are cooked by other methods, is less of a problem.

Birds present many opportunities for introducing new flavours. As well as putting herbs, spices or vegetables in the cavity, try a few sprigs of lavender (use the Old English variety for most effect), elderflowers or scented rose petals. Flavourings can even be inserted under the skin of both whole birds and portions, though this will slow down the rate of cooking and will be particularly noticeable when cooking the latter.

The length of time required for cooking poultry and game depends not only on the structure and texture of the meat but, whether it is being cooked on or off the bone or with or without other ingredients, and how well done you prefer it.

I prefer to use chicken breasts that are off the bone and where 'chicken breasts' are specified in the recipes and in the chart, it refers to the whole breast, not just the fillet or 'suprême'. The portion containing the bone I've called the 'chicken breast portion'. The cooking times in both the chart and the recipes also include 'resting' time when the heat and juices become evenly distributed throughout the flesh.

Meat	Weight	Steaming time
Chicken		
whole	1.5 kg / 3 lb	50–60 mins
breast, skinned	150 g / 5 oz	7 mins a side
leg, skinned	250 g / 9 oz	30 mins
thigh	150 g / 5 oz	6–7 mins a side
wing minus tip	115 g / 4 oz	15 mins
Duck breast, skinned	150 g / 5 oz	4 mins a side
Guinea fowl	1 kg / 2 lb 2 oz	30–35 mins
Hare	fillet	3–5 mins
Partridge	450 g / 1 lb	20 mins
Pheasant	1 kg / 2 lb 2 oz	25–30 mins
Pigeon	400 g / 14 oz	30–33 mins
Poussin	350 g / 12 oz	20 mins
Quail		15–17 mins
Rabbit, saddle	250 g / 9 oz	4½–5 mins
hind leg	150 g / 5 oz	4½–5 mins
Spring chicken	800 g / 1¾ lb	33 mins
Turkey fillet, skinned	150 g / 5 oz	4–4½ mins a side
Venison steaks	150 g / 5 oz	1½ mins a side
Woodcock	375 g / 13 oz	12 mins

STUFFED BONED
POUSSINS
SERVES 4

The poussins can be served more simply, if preferred, while still in
their parcels.

---

115 g/4 oz WATERCRESS LEAVES AND FINE STEMS

225 g/8 oz COOKED YOUNG BROAD BEANS, REMOVED
FROM THEIR OUTER SKINS IF TOUGH

115 g/4 oz RICOTTA CHEESE

1 EGG YOLK

SQUEEZE OF LEMON JUICE

SALT AND FRESHLY GROUND BLACK PEPPER

4 × 400 g/14 oz POUSSINS

SMALL SPRIGS OF SUMMER SAVORY OR PARSLEY,
FOR GARNISH

Blanch the watercress for 45 seconds, refresh under cold running
water, drain well and pat dry, then purée with the broad beans, ricotta
and egg yolk. Add the lemon juice and season to taste.

Cut through the poussins' legs at the first joint, then place the birds
breast downwards and cut through the back bones with a small sharp
knife. Cut away the flesh from the carcass using short, sharp strokes
and taking care not to pierce the skin. Cut through the thigh bones but
leave the lower leg and wing bones in place.

Divide the broad bean purée between the birds, spreading it evenly.
Tuck the skin over the filling, reshape the birds and tie them securely
but not too tightly with string. Place each bird on a large sheet of
seasoned greaseproof paper. Enclose the birds loosely but seal tightly.
Steam for about 12 minutes.

Leaving the poussins in their parcels, remove from the heat and
keep warm for 3–4 minutes.

Carefully lift the poussins from the paper, allowing any juices to drain off, and cut the birds into neat slices. Re-form on warmed plates and spoon the juices from the parcels, re-heated if necessary, over the poussins. Garnish with small sprigs of summer savory or parsley.

POUSSINS WITH SHALLOTS, BASIL AND LEMON

SERVES 4

The combination of basil, lemon, shallots and garlic add flavour to this otherwise mild meat.

SALT AND FRESHLY GROUND WHITE PEPPER
4 × 350 g/12 oz POUSSINS
1 CLOVE OF GARLIC, CRUSHED
4 SHALLOTS, FINELY CHOPPED
FINELY GRATED RIND AND JUICE OF 4 LEMONS
6 SPRIGS OF BASIL
450 ml/16 fl oz CHICKEN STOCK, SEE PAGE 21
4 TABLESPOONS DOUBLE CREAM
50 g/2 oz UNSALTED BUTTER, DICED

Season the poussins inside and out. Add the garlic, shallots, lemon rind and juice and stalks of the basil sprigs to the stock. Steam the poussins over this liquor for about 20 minutes, turning the birds over half-way through. Remove from the heat and keep warm.

Boil the steaming liquor until reduced to 225 ml/8 fl oz. Pass through a sieve and reheat in a clean pan. Stir in the cream and boil for a minute or two. Reduce the heat to very low and gradually swirl in the butter, making sure each piece is fully incorporated before adding the next.

Taste and adjust the seasoning, if necessary. Keep warm over a very low heat – do not allow to boil.

Serve the poussins with the sauce poured over. Garnish with the leaves from the basil sprigs.

POUSSINS WITH SHERRY SAUCE

SERVES 4

4 LEEKS, TRIMMED BUT INCLUDING SOME GREEN PART

150 ml / ¼ PINT DRY SHERRY

2 STICKS OF CELERY, CHOPPED

6 SPRIGS OF PARSLEY, ROUGHLY CHOPPED

1 BAY LEAF

2 CLOVES

500 ml / 18 fl oz CHICKEN STOCK, SEE PAGE 21

8 SMALL ONIONS OR SHALLOTS

4 POUSSINS, ABOUT 350 g / 12 oz EACH

50 g / 2 oz UNSALTED BUTTER, DICED

SALT AND FRESHLY GROUND BLACK PEPPER

Keeping the white and green parts of the leeks separate, slice them coarsely. Lay the white part on the bottom of a steaming basket or colander or on a rack. Add the green parts of the leeks, with the sherry, celery, parsley, bay leaf and cloves to the stock and bring to the boil.

Put 2 small onions or shallots inside the cavity of each poussin then steam over the flavoured stock for about 20 minutes. Remove the poussins and white part of leek from the heat and keep warm.

Strain the stock and then boil until reduced to 150 ml / ¼ pint. Turn down the heat to very low and gradually whisk in the butter, making sure each piece is fully incorporated before adding the next. Season to taste.

To serve, pour some of the sauce on to 4 warmed plates, place the poussins with the white part of the leeks on top, and pour the remaining sauce over.

CHICKEN THIGHS WITH AUBERGINE SAUCE

SERVES 4

Ground coriander gives the chicken a subtle taste which goes well with the flavour of the sauce. The sauce and thighs together are quite filling, but hearty eaters may prefer to have two chicken thighs each.

---

2 × 225 g/8 oz AUBERGINES
1 TABLESPOON GROUND CORIANDER
300 ml/½ PINT CHICKEN STOCK, SEE PAGE 21
4 CHICKEN THIGHS, ABOUT 150 g/5 oz EACH, SKINNED
1 SHALLOT, FINELY CHOPPED
1¼ TEASPOONS GROUND CUMIN

20 g/¾ oz WHITE PART OF SPRING ONIONS,
FINELY CHOPPED
2 TABLESPOONS FROMAGE BLANC
SALT AND FRESHLY GROUND BLACK PEPPER
PAPRIKA PEPPER AND FINELY CHOPPED PARSLEY,
FOR GARNISH

Cut the aubergines in half lengthways. Score the surfaces with a sharp knife. Add the coriander to the stock then steam the aubergines over this liquid for 8–10 minutes, until tender. When the aubergines are cool enough to handle, scoop out the flesh and reserve.

Steam the chicken thighs over the stock for 13 minutes, until just cooked. Remove the basket or colander from the pan and keep the chicken warm.

Cook the shallot in the steaming liquid until it has almost completely evaporated, then add to the aubergine flesh with the ground cumin. Purée this mixture until smooth. Transfer to a medium-sized saucepan, add the spring onions and reheat gently. Stir in the fromage blanc and season, if necessary.

Serve the chicken thighs with the sauce poured around and garnish with paprika and finely chopped parsley.

CHICKEN WITH LETTUCE AND AVOCADO SAUCE

SERVES 4

In the absence of fresh basil use a little pesto sauce to spread in the chicken breasts instead.

———————

4 TEASPOONS FINELY CHOPPED BASIL
100 g/3½ oz SOFT CHEESE
4 CHICKEN BREASTS, ABOUT 150 g/5 oz EACH, SKINNED
SALT AND FRESHLY GROUND BLACK PEPPER
6 TABLESPOONS MEDIUM-BODIED DRY WHITE WINE
150 g/5 oz ICEBERG LETTUCE LEAVES, SHREDDED
½ A RIPE AVOCADO, WEIGHING ABOUT 300 g/10 oz

———————

Mix together the basil and soft cheese. Divide this mixture between the chicken breasts, spreading it in the natural pocket formed by the smaller fillet and main part of the breast. Place each breast, fillet uppermost, on a piece of foil large enough to enclose it completely. Turn up the edges of the foil. Season lightly, then pour 1½ tablespoons wine over each breast. Fold the foil loosely over the breasts and seal the edges tightly together. Steam for about 17 minutes. Remove the foil parcels from the heat, open them up and carefully pour the juices into a small saucepan. Fold the foil back over the breasts to keep them warm. Add the lettuce to the juices and simmer for a minute or so, then transfer this mixture to a food processor or blender. Remove the stone from the avocado and scoop out the flesh into the food processor. Purée to leave a sauce with some texture. If you do not own a food processor or blender, pass the mixture through a sieve.

Return the sauce to the saucepan and reheat. Taste, adjust the seasoning and add a little extra wine or some dry white vermouth if the consistency is too thick.

Serve the breasts with the sauce poured around.

CHICKEN WITH LEEKS
SERVES 4

This sauce can be made with either cream or strained Greek yoghurt – although the consistency and taste will be different, the end result will be equally as good.

---

65 g/2½ oz WHITE PART OF LEEK, SLICED
50 g/2 oz YOUNG SPINACH LEAVES
4 CHICKEN BREASTS, ABOUT 150 g/5 oz EACH
400 ml/14 fl oz CHICKEN STOCK, SEE PAGE 21
65 ml/2½ fl oz DRY WHITE VERMOUTH (OPTIONAL)
115 ml/4 fl oz DOUBLE CREAM OR GREEK YOGHURT
2 EGG YOLKS
SALT AND FRESHLY GROUND BLACK PEPPER
SMALL SPRIGS OF HERBS, PREFERABLY CONTAINING FLOWERS, FOR GARNISH

Lay the leeks and spinach leaves in the bottom of a steaming basket or colander or on a rack. Place the chicken breasts on top and steam over the chicken stock for about 7 minutes each side.

Meanwhile, boil the vermouth, if used, until reduced to 1 tablespoon.

When the chicken is cooked, remove the basket, colander or rack from the pan and keep the meat warm. Add the leeks and spinach to the steaming liquor, stir into the reduced vermouth, if used, or into a clean pan, and boil until reduced to 115 ml/4 fl oz. Purée with the cream or yoghurt and heat very gently. Whisk the egg yolks in a small bowl placed over a saucepan of hot water until light and fluffy, then gradually whisk in the leek mixture. Season with salt and pepper.

Remove the skin from the chicken, then either slice the breasts or leave them whole. To serve, pour the sauce on to 4 warmed plates and arrange the chicken on top. Garnish with small sprigs of herbs.

CHICKEN WITH
VEGETABLES AND HERBS
SERVES 4

---

2 LEEKS, CUT INTO FINE STRIPS
2 YOUNG CARROTS, CUT INTO FINE SHREDS
1 BAY LEAF, BROKEN
2 SPRIGS OF THYME
2 SAGE LEAVES
4 CHICKEN QUARTERS, SKINNED
SALT AND FRESHLY GROUND BLACK PEPPER
LEMON JUICE
4 TABLESPOONS MEDIUM-BODIED DRY WHITE WINE
(OPTIONAL)
CHOPPED HERBS, FOR GARNISH

Line a steaming basket or large colander with foil so that it comes well up the sides. On to this place the leeks, carrots and herbs. Season the chicken quarters with salt, pepper and a good squeeze of lemon juice, and lay them on the bed of vegetables and herbs. Sprinkle with the wine, if used.

Steam for about 25–30 minutes, depending on the size of the portions, until the chicken is tender, and turning the portions over about half-way through.

Remove the chicken from the basket or colander and take the herbs out of the vegetables.

Serve the chicken with the vegetables. Pour the cooking juices over and sprinkle with fresh herbs.

CHICKEN WITH TARRAGON

SERVES 4

For a more simple dish leave out the sauce.

---

12 SPRIGS OF TARRAGON

4 CHICKEN BREASTS, ABOUT 175 g/6 oz EACH,
SKINNED

150 ml/¼ PINT MEDIUM-BODIED DRY WHITE WINE

300 ml/½ PINT CHICKEN STOCK, SEE PAGE 21

25 g/1 oz UNSALTED BUTTER, DICED

2 LARGE TOMATOES, SKINNED AND SEEDS
REMOVED, CHOPPED

SALT AND FRESHLY GROUND BLACK PEPPER

Lay half the sprigs of tarragon in the bottom of a steaming basket
or colander. Place the chicken breasts on top. Sprinkle over the
remaining tarragon sprigs and cover with a sheet of greaseproof paper.
Add the wine to the stock and steam the chicken over this liquid for

about 14 minutes, or until just tender. Remove the basket or colander from the pan and keep the chicken warm.

Boil the stock until reduced to 100 ml/3½ fl oz. Lightly whisk in the butter, making sure each piece is incorporated before adding the next. Add the tomatoes and season to taste.

Remove the tarragon from the breasts. Slice the breasts, if preferred, then serve with the sauce poured around.

CHICKEN BREASTS WITH FRESH CORIANDER SAUCE

SERVES 4

LEAVES AND STEMS FROM A SMALL BUNCH (ABOUT
5 g/scant ¼ oz) FRESH CORIANDER
4 CHICKEN BREASTS, SKINNED
300 ml/½ PINT CHICKEN STOCK, SEE PAGE 21
75 ml/3 fl oz DRY WHITE VERMOUTH
1 SHALLOT, FINELY CHOPPED
225 g/8 oz FROMAGE BLANC
SALT AND FRESHLY GROUND BLACK PEPPER

Place about a third of the coriander leaves and stems in the bottom of a steaming basket or colander. Lay the chicken breasts on top, then steam over the stock for about 3–4 minutes each side. Remove the basket or colander from the pan, keep the chicken warm and reserve the coriander.

Meanwhile, in a separate saucepan, simmer the vermouth with the shallot until the liquid has almost completely evaporated. Stir the stock into the shallot mixture and boil until reduced to 25 ml/1 fl oz.

Purée the reserved coriander with the fromage blanc.

Reduce the heat beneath the reduced stock and stir in the coriander purée. Heat through gently, stirring with a wooden spoon – do not allow to boil. Season to taste. Cover and remove from the heat.

To serve, cut the chicken into slices, pour some of the sauce on to 4 warmed plates, place the chicken on top and trickle the remaining sauce over. Garnish with the remaining coriander leaves.

CHICKEN ON A BED OF GARLIC AND PARSLEY

SERVES 4

A simple dish which can be served with or without the sauce.

---

5 CLOVES OF GARLIC, PEELED

8–10 LARGE SPRIGS OF PARSLEY

SALT AND FRESHLY GROUND BLACK PEPPER

4 CHICKEN PORTIONS, SKINNED

1 SHALLOT, FINELY CHOPPED

450 ml/16 fl oz CHICKEN STOCK, SEE PAGE 21

2 TABLESPOONS SHERRY VINEGAR

APPROX 1 TEASPOON TOMATO PURÉE

APPROX 2 TEASPOONS FRENCH MUSTARD

40 ml/1½ fl oz WHIPPING CREAM OR 40 g/1½ oz
FROMAGE BLANC

25 g/1 oz UNSALTED BUTTER, DICED

SPRIGS OF PARSLEY, FOR GARNISH

Finely chop together the garlic and parsley. With half of this mixture, make a bed in the bottom of a steaming basket or colander. Season the chicken portions and lay them on the bed. Spread the remaining parsley and garlic mixture over the chicken. Add the shallot to the stock and steam the chicken over this liquid for about 5 minutes each side, depending on the size of the portions. Remove the basket or colander from the pan and keep the chicken and parsley mixture warm.

In a medium-sized saucepan, boil the vinegar until almost completely evaporated. Add the stock and shallot to the reduced vinegar and boil until reduced to 175 ml/6 fl oz, then gradually whisk in the tomato purée, mustard, cream or fromage blanc. Reduce the heat to very low, and swirl in the butter, making sure each piece is incorporated before adding the next. Taste and adjust the seasoning and balance of flavours if necessary.

Serve the sauce poured around the chicken breasts and garnish with sprigs of parsley.

CHICKEN WITH DRIED APRICOTS AND ALMONDS

SERVES 4

The sauce, which is very simple to prepare, adds a real touch of distinction, but for a more straightforward dish, simply cook the breasts with the ground almond mixture, over seasoned or flavoured water.

---

8 DRIED APRICOTS, SOAKED OVERNIGHT IN
BRANDY, WHISKY OR WHITE WINE
20 g/¾ oz GROUND ALMONDS
SMALL PINCH OF GROUND CINNAMON
SALT AND FRESHLY GROUND BLACK PEPPER
4 CHICKEN BREASTS, ABOUT 150 g/5 oz EACH, SKINNED
200 ml/7 fl oz FULL-BODIED DRY WHITE WINE
400 ml/14 fl oz CHICKEN STOCK, SEE PAGE 21
25 g/1 oz UNSALTED BUTTER, DICED

Roughly chop the apricots, add the ground almonds and mix to a smooth paste. Flavour very lightly with cinnamon, then add a little salt and pepper. Divide this mixture between the natural pockets in the chicken breasts and press the sides gently together.

Add the wine to the stock and steam the chicken over this liquid for about 16–18 minutes. Remove the chicken from the heat and keep warm.

Boil the steaming liquor until reduced to 225 ml / 8 fl oz. Reduce the heat to very low and gradually swirl in the butter, making sure each piece is incorporated before adding the next. Adjust the seasoning, if necessary. Slice the breasts, or leave them whole, whichever you prefer, and serve with the sauce poured over.

CHICKEN WITH LIME

SERVES 4

If neither lemon verbena nor thyme are available, parsley can be used instead. If you don't have any chicken stock already made, make a simple one by simmering the chicken skin and bones with a chopped shallot or small onion, a small chopped carrot, a few white peppercorns and a bouquet garni, for about 45 minutes. Sliced courgettes and new potatoes steamed in their jackets make good accompaniments.

---

4 CHICKEN BREAST PORTIONS, SKINNED

3 LIMES, THINLY SLICED

1 SPRIG OF MARJORAM

1 SPRIG OF LEMON VERBENA OR LEMON THYME

300 ml / ½ PINT CHICKEN STOCK, SEE PAGE 21

JUICE OF 2 LIMES

3 EGG YOLKS

GROUND ALLSPICE

SALT AND FRESHLY GROUND WHITE PEPPER

SPRIGS OF LEMON VERBENA OR LEMON THYME OR MARJORAM, FOR GARNISH

Cut away in one piece the chicken breasts from the carcasses and wing bones.

Arrange half the lime slices in four lines in the bottom of a steaming basket or on a rack. Lay the breasts on the lime and cover with the remaining slices. Add the marjoram and lemon verbena or lemon thyme to the stock and steam the chicken over this liquid for about 7 minutes each side, depending on the size of the portions. Remove the basket or rack from the pan and keep the chicken warm.

Measure the stock – you will need about 200 ml/7 fl oz. If necessary, boil to reduce, or make up with water. Bring the stock almost to the boil. In a large bowl, whisk together the lime juice and egg yolks, then gradually stir in the hot stock. Pour back into the pan and cook over a very low heat, stirring constantly, until the sauce thickens. Do not allow it to boil. (If you are worried about the sauce curdling, make it in a bowl placed over a saucepan of hot water.) Add ground allspice and season with salt and pepper to taste.

Remove the lime slices from the chicken. Slice the breasts or leave them whole – whichever you prefer. Serve with some of the sauce poured around and a trickle poured over each breast. Garnish with sprigs of lemon verbena or lemon thyme or marjoram.

CHICKEN BLANQUETTE

SERVES 4

The celeriac looks more impressive if cut into small torpedo shapes. Young broad beans are a good accompanying vegetable as neither their colour nor flavour dominate the delicacy of the dish.

BOUQUET GARNI OF 2 BAY LEAVES, 6 PARSLEY STALKS, SPRIG OF ROSEMARY AND 12 CHIVES

425 ml/¾ PINT CHICKEN STOCK, SEE PAGE 21 PREFERABLY JELLIED

8 SMALL PEELED ONIONS, ABOUT 15 g/½ oz EACH

300 g/10 oz PEELED CELERIAC, CUT INTO STRIPS APPROX 1.25 × 3 cm/½ × 1¼ in

450 g / 1 lb SKINNED CHICKEN BREAST, CUT INTO
PIECES APPROX 3.75 × 8.25 cm / 1½ × 3½ in

150 ml / ¼ PINT WHIPPING CREAM

2 EGG YOLKS

15 g / ½ oz UNSALTED BUTTER, DICED

SALT AND FRESHLY GROUND WHITE PEPPER

LEMON JUICE

FRESH BAY LEAVES OR SMALL SPRIGS OF PARSLEY,
FOR GARNISH

Add the bouquet garni to the stock then steam the onions and celeriac over this liquid for about 4 minutes. Add the chicken and cook for 4 minutes, turning it over about half-way through. Remove the vegetables and chicken from the heat and keep warm.

Boil the stock until reduced to 115 ml / 4 fl oz. Remove the bouquet garni and stir in the cream. Boil briefly, then reduce the heat. In a bowl, mix a little of the stock with the egg yolks, then pour the egg yolk mixture back into the stock.

Heat gently, stirring with a wooden spoon until the sauce begins to thicken – do not allow to boil. Stir in the butter, season with salt and pepper and add a little lemon juice to lift the flavour.

Gently fold the chicken pieces into the sauce and serve with the celeriac and onions. Garnish with herbs.

CHICKEN BREASTS WITH MILD GARLIC SAUCE

SERVES 2

The sauce in this recipe is light and delicately flavoured with just a hint of garlic. Serve with a colourful vegetable and either new potatoes steamed in their jackets or sliced old potatoes.

---

5 LARGE, FRESH CLOVES OF GARLIC, CRUSHED

300 ml/½ PINT CHICKEN STOCK, SEE PAGE 21

2 SKINNED CHICKEN BREASTS, ABOUT
115–150 g/4–5 oz EACH

SALT AND FRESHLY GROUND WHITE PEPPER

50 g/2 oz FROMAGE FRAIS

Simmer the garlic cloves gently in the stock for 10 minutes. Then steam the chicken breasts over this liquid for about 8 minutes, turning them over half-way through. Remove the chicken from the heat, season lightly and keep warm.

Purée the stock and garlic cloves, return to the pan and boil until reduced to 100 ml/3½ fl oz. Reduce the heat to very low and stir in the fromage frais. Taste and adjust the seasoning, if necessary.

Pour the sauce over the chicken breasts and serve hot or cold.

COUNTRY CHICKEN

SERVES 4

The vegetables and herbs placed inside the chicken are variable. As
an alternative to those given in the recipe, you can use an onion,
shallot or spring onions, carrot, celery, mushrooms, rosemary or
sage, marjoram, fennel or dill, and chives. If you do not have any
ready-made chicken stock, steam the meat over seasoned water
flavoured with vegetables and herbs.

Add extra flavour to the steaming liquid by pouring in some dry
white wine.

1.5 kg/3 lb CHICKEN

FRESHLY GROUND BLACK PEPPER

1 LEEK, SLICED

1 SMALL LEMON, QUARTERED

BOUQUET GARNI OF A BAY LEAF, SPRIG OF PARSLEY,
AND SMALL SPRIG EACH OF TARRAGON AND THYME

450 ml/16 fl oz CHICKEN STOCK, SEE PAGE 21

25 g/1 oz UNSALTED BUTTER, DICED

FINELY CHOPPED PARSLEY, TARRAGON OR THYME,
FOR GARNISH

Sprinkle the inside of the chicken with black pepper, then place the
leeks, lemon and bouquet garni in the cavity. Steam the chicken over
the stock for about 55 minutes. Remove from the heat and keep warm.

Boil the stock until reduced to 150 ml/¼ pint then, over a low heat,
gradually swirl in the butter, making sure each piece is incorporated
before adding the next.

Carve the chicken and serve with the sauce poured around. Garnish
with a little parsley, tarragon or thyme.

SAFFRON-SCENTED WHOLE CHICKEN

SERVES 4

The taste of saffron adds such a sense of luxury that I never hesitate to serve it for a special meal. But, make sure you buy genuine saffron threads and not powdered saffron, which is a very inferior substitute.

¼ TEASPOON SAFFRON THREADS

1 TEASPOON SALT

40 g/1½ oz UNSALTED BUTTER, SOFTENED

1.5 kg/3 lb CHICKEN

1 SMALL CARROT, QUARTERED

1 SHALLOT, HALVED

1 SMALL STICK OF CELERY

BOUQUET GARNI OF A SPRIG OF THYME, 2 SPRIGS OF PARSLEY, A SPRIG OF CHERVIL AND A SMALL SPRIG OF TARRAGON

SPRIGS OF CHERVIL, FOR GARNISH

Pound the saffron with the salt, leave to stand for 10 minutes, then mix with the butter. Rub thoroughly into the skin of the chicken. Add the vegetables and bouquet garni to a steamer or large pan containing 400 ml/14 fl oz water. Steam the chicken over this liquid for about an hour. Remove from the heat and keep warm.

Strain the steaming liquor. Taste to see if it needs to be reduced to concentrate the flavours or if it needs a little seasoning.

Slice the chicken and serve accompanied by the juices, and garnished with sprigs of chervil.

SPRING CHICKEN WITH ELDERFLOWERS AND ELDERBERRY SAUCE

SERVES 4

The elderflowers, in bloom in June and early July, when the first gooseberries are just ripe, give the delicately-flavoured flesh of spring chicken a subtle flavour. Chicken can be cooked in the same way and is particularly good cold – ideal for sunny days and picnics.

---

2 SPRING CHICKENS, ABOUT 800 g/1¾ lb DRAWN WEIGHT

HANDFUL OF ELDERFLOWER SPRIGS

400 ml/14 fl oz CHICKEN STOCK, SEE PAGE 21

1–2 TEASPOONS ELDERBERRY JELLY

SQUEEZE OF LEMON JUICE

20 RIPE GOOSEBERRIES

SALT AND FRESHLY GROUND BLACK PEPPER

7 g/¼ oz UNSALTED BUTTER

SPRIGS OF ELDERFLOWERS, FOR GARNISH

Fill the cavity of each spring chicken with elderflowers then steam over the stock for about 33 minutes. Remove from the heat and keep warm.

Boil the steaming liquor until reduced to 175 ml/6 fl oz. Pour in the juices from the chicken and reduce again to 175 ml/6 fl oz. Stir in a little elderberry jelly and a squeeze of lemon juice.

Reduce the heat, add the gooseberries and warm through. Using a slotted spoon remove the gooseberries and keep warm. Season the sauce and swirl in the butter. Keep warm over a low heat.

Carve off the breasts of the chicken, remove the skin from the legs and place one breast and one leg on each plate. Serve the sauce poured over, add the gooseberries, and garnish with sprigs of elderflowers.

TURKEY IN CITRUS MARINADE

SERVES 4

This is one of the best ways I have come across for preparing turkey that is to be served cold, as the flesh stays moist, succulent and tasty during cooking, instead of drying out.

---

4 TURKEY BREAST FILLETS
300 ml/½ PINT CHICKEN STOCK, SEE PAGE 21
2–3 SPRING ONIONS, DEPENDING ON SIZE, CHOPPED
50 ml/2 fl oz DRY VERMOUTH
50 ml/2 fl oz BIANCO VERMOUTH
1½ TABLESPOONS GRATED ORANGE RIND
6 TABLESPOONS FRESH ORANGE JUICE
2 TABLESPOONS LEMON JUICE
SALT AND FRESHLY GROUND BLACK PEPPER
1 TABLESPOON CHOPPED PARSLEY
ORANGE WEDGES, SPRING ONIONS AND SPRIGS OF
PARSLEY, FOR GARNISH

Steam the turkey over the stock for about 8 minutes each side. Transfer the fillets to a shallow non-metallic dish that they just fit in a single layer.

Add the spring onions to the stock and boil briskly until the stock has almost completely evaporated. Add the vermouths and orange rind and boil again for about 20 seconds. Stir in the orange juice and lemon juice and boil again for about a minute. Season with salt and pepper, add the parsley and pour over the turkey.

When the marinade has cooled, turn the turkey over. Cover and leave at room temperature for about 6 hours, turning the turkey over occasionally.

Serve with any remaining marinade and garnish with orange wedges, spring onions and parsley.

TURKEY ROLL

SERVES 4–6

The Red Pepper Sauce (see page 183) is not vital to the enjoyment of this dish but it adds colour and enhances the flavour of the turkey.

---

10 SAVOY CABBAGE LEAVES

25 g/1 oz DRIED PORCINI OR CÈPES MUSHROOMS, SOAKED IN WARM WATER FOR 2 HOURS

1 × 575 g/1¼ lb BONED TURKEY BREAST, FAT AND SKIN DISCARDED

100 g/3½ oz COOKED CRACKED WHEAT, LIGHTLY SEASONED

75 g/3 oz THINLY SLICED BLACK FOREST OR WESTPHALIAN HAM

1 CLOVE OF GARLIC, FINELY CHOPPED

1 MEDIUM ONION, THINLY SLICED

1 LARGE RED PEPPER, CUT INTO 1.25 cm/½ in WIDE STRIPS

CHICKEN STOCK FOR STEAMING, SEE PAGE 21

RED PEPPER SAUCE, TO SERVE (SEE PAGE 183)

Steam the cabbage leaves for 2–3 minutes until just tender. Cut out and discard the raised part of the veins.

Drain the mushrooms, squeeze out excess moisture, then chop them, discarding any hard parts.

Make a cut along the length of the turkey but not quite all the way through to give a large rectangle. Sandwich the turkey between two pieces of greaseproof paper and beat to about 8 mm/¼ in thick.

Lay out 8 of the cabbage leaves, overlapping them slightly, to give a rectangle about 37.5 × 55 cm/15 × 22 in. Place the turkey on the leaves. Spread the cracked wheat on top, then cover with the ham, garlic, onion and mushrooms. Arrange the red pepper strips at one short end. Fold in one long side of the cabbage leaves. Starting at the end with the peppers, roll up the cabbage and turkey. Patch any gaps with the remaining cabbage leaves, if necessary. Wrap the roll in greaseproof paper, twist the ends together and secure with string or metal ties. Steam over the stock for about 40 minutes, until just springy to the touch.

Leave to cool for 5 minutes then unwrap and cut into 2 cm / ¾ in slices. Serve with the Red Pepper Sauce.

TURKEY WITH MUSTARD TOPPING
SERVES 4

Although the turkey is cooked with mustard, the result is not a hot dish. Whole grain mustard is much milder than other types, and the flavour is further mellowed during steaming.

———

6 TABLESPOONS WHOLE GRAIN MUSTARD
4 TURKEY BREAST FILLETS, ABOUT 150 g / 5 oz EACH
150 ml / ¼ PINT DRY SHERRY
450 ml / 16 fl oz TURKEY STOCK, SEE PAGE 21
50 g / 2 oz UNSALTED BUTTER, DICED
SALT AND FRESHLY GROUND BLACK PEPPER

———

Spread the mustard over one side of the turkey fillets, then in a steamer or large pan, boil the sherry until reduced to 25 ml / 1 fl oz. Add the stock and steam the turkey mustard side uppermost over this liquid for about 8–9 minutes, depending on the size and thickness of the fillets. Remove from the heat and keep warm.

Boil the steaming liquor until reduced to 150 ml / ¼ pint. Reduce the heat to very low then gradually swirl in the butter, making sure each piece is fully incorporated before adding the next. Season with salt and pepper.

Serve the turkey with the sauce poured around.

TEA-SCENTED DUCK
SERVES 4

Orange Pekoe tea adds a subtle flavour that enhances that of the duck.

---

2 TABLESPOONS ORANGE PEKOE TEA
4 DUCK BREASTS, SKINNED
SALT

In a steamer or large pan, boil 300 ml / ½ pint water and add the tea. Steam the duck breasts over the tea for about 4 minutes each side. Season the duck with a very little salt. Turn the heat off, and keep the breasts warm for a few minutes before serving with a simple crisp green salad.

DUCK WITH
APPLE-CLOVE SAUCE
SERVES 4

Four dried cloves should be sufficient to give a hint of flavour to this dish, but if the cloves have been stored for a while, an extra one may be necessary. An equally delicious sauce can be made using fromage frais instead of cream, but after stirring it in, do not boil. The sauce is also very good served cold.

---

300 ml / ½ PINT APPLE JUICE
50 ml / 2 fl oz DRY VERMOUTH (OPTIONAL)
4 CLOVES
1 LARGE COX'S ORANGE PIPPIN APPLE
4 DUCK BREASTS, ABOUT 150 g / 5 oz EACH, SKINNED
115 ml / 4 fl oz DOUBLE CREAM
15 g / ½ oz UNSALTED BUTTER, DICED
SALT AND FRESHLY GROUND BLACK PEPPER
LEMON JUICE

Pour the apple juice, vermouth, if used, and cloves into a steamer or large pan.

Peel and core the apple, then cut into 1.25 cm / ½ in thick slices. Place in a steaming basket or colander or on a rack. Arrange the duck breasts in a single layer on top and steam for about 7 minutes. Turn the duck breasts over half-way through – they should be pink in the centre. Remove from the heat and keep warm.

Boil the steaming liquor until reduced to about 65 ml / 2½ fl oz. Remove the cloves, stir in the cream and simmer until slightly thickened. Lower the heat and swirl in the butter. Season with salt, pepper and a little lemon juice, to taste. Keep warm or leave to cool.

Slice the breasts, reform the shape and serve with the sauce underneath and the apples on top.

DUCK WITH LEMON GRASS

SERVES 4

Lemon grass, a fragrant lemon-scented spice often used in Indonesian cooking, is now available from some supermarkets.

3–4 BULBS OF LEMON GRASS, DEPENDING ON SIZE
4 DUCK BREASTS, ABOUT 150 g/5 oz EACH, SKINNED
350 ml/12 fl oz CHICKEN STOCK, SEE PAGE 21
150 ml/¼ PINT MEDIUM-BODIED DRY WHITE WINE
125 g/4½ oz FROMAGE FRAIS
SALT AND FRESHLY GROUND BLACK PEPPER
SPRIGS OF CHERVIL, FOR GARNISH

Chop the bulbs of lemon grass then pound them in a mortar mixed with a teaspoon or so of warm water. Leave to soak for about 15 minutes until softened, then pound them again. Spread this mixture over the duck breasts and leave in a cool place for 2–3 hours.

Lift the duck breasts out of the marinade and steam over the stock for 7 minutes, until pink in the centre.

Meanwhile boil the wine until reduced to 65 ml/2½ fl oz.

Remove the duck from the heat and keep warm.

Add the steaming liquor to the reduced wine and boil until reduced again to 65 ml/2½ fl oz. Reduce the heat to very low then stir in the fromage frais. Heat very gently, stirring, and do not allow it to boil. Season with salt and pepper.

To serve, arrange the duck breasts on the sauce and garnish with sprigs of chervil.

QUAILS WITH BACON AND SAGE

SERVES 4

If possible, buy quails that have their 'innards' included so the livers can be wrapped into the bacon rolls. If, like me, you prefer to use just the lean 'eye' of the bacon, you will need double the number of slices.

---

115 ml/4 fl oz MEDIUM-BODIED RED WINE

50 ml/2 fl oz GIN

SALT AND FRESHLY GROUND BLACK PEPPER

24 JUNIPER BERRIES, LIGHTLY TOASTED

8 QUAILS

10 MEDIUM-SIZED SAGE LEAVES

4 SMALL, THIN SLICES OF BACK BACON, PREFERABLY LIGHTLY SMOKED, HALVED ACROSS

450 ml/16 fl oz BROWN VEAL STOCK, SEE PAGE 25

25 g/1 oz UNSALTED BUTTER, DICED

Mix together the red wine and gin, and season lightly with salt and pepper. Put 2 juniper berries inside each quail, then place the quails in a non-metallic dish that holds them snugly together. Pour the red wine over, cover and leave to marinate for up to 12 hours, turning the birds occasionally.

Remove the quails and reserve the marinade.

Lay a sage leaf on each piece of bacon and roll the bacon up round it. Place one roll inside each bird. Add the remaining sage leaves, juniper berries and the reserved marinade to the stock, cover and simmer gently for 15 minutes. Steam the quails over the liquor for about 15–17 minutes, so they remain slightly pink. Remove the quails from the heat and keep warm.

Take the sage leaves out of the steaming liquor. Boil until reduced to 150 ml/¼ pint. Remove the juniper berries then, over a very low heat, gradually swirl in the butter, making sure each piece is incorporated before adding the next. Taste and adjust the seasoning, if necessary.

Remove the bacon rolls from the quails. These can either be sliced into rings, or left whole. To serve, pour the sauce on to 4 warmed plates, place the quails on top and arrange the bacon rolls beside them.

FRAGRANT PIGEONS

SERVES 4

The majority of pigeons available from supermarkets and good butchers are bred, so do not tend to be as tough as wild birds. However, if you are cooking a wild bird, you may need to increase the cooking time to tenderize the flesh.
Port colours the birds slightly and adds richness to the juices but, if you prefer, just use white wine. Using game stock, or any other stock that you have available, also adds richness to the sauce as juices that condense on the lid of the steamer will drip on to the birds and into the foil.

———

2 TEASPOONS GROUND CINNAMON

1 TEASPOON GROUND GINGER

1 TABLESPOON GROUND CORIANDER

1 TEASPOON MIXED SPICE

4 TEASPOONS CLEAR HONEY

4 PIGEONS, ABOUT 350 g/12 oz EACH

40 g/1½ oz DRIED APRICOTS, CHOPPED, SOAKED OVERNIGHT

4 TABLESPOONS FULL-BODIED DRY WHITE WINE

4 TABLESPOONS PORT (OPTIONAL)

GAME STOCK FOR STEAMING (OPTIONAL), SEE PAGE 22

SALT AND FRESHLY GROUND BLACK PEPPER

LEMON JUICE

———

Mix together the spices and honey, then rub into the skin of the pigeons. Divide about a quarter of the apricots between the 4 pigeons and put into the cavities. Cover and leave in a cool place for a couple of hours.

Line a steaming basket or large colander with a sheet of foil, but leave room for the steam to go between the foil and the sides of the container. Place the pigeons on the foil, add the remaining apricots and the wine and port, if used. Cover and steam over the stock, or seasoned water, for about 30–35 minutes or until the birds are just cooked. Remove the birds from the basket or colander and keep warm.

Carefully pour the juices and the apricots out of the foil into a separate pan and boil until slightly syrupy. Season with salt and pepper and add a little lemon juice, if necessary.

Serve the pigeons with the juices and apricots poured over.

PARTRIDGE WITH GIROLLES AND MADEIRA SAUCE

SERVES 4

Young, or fairly young, birds are best for this dish. Girolles are deliciously flavoured wild mushrooms that are normally available during the autumn, though chefs are now getting them at other times of the year. If you cannot buy girolles, use oyster mushrooms, which can be bought at many supermarkets. Broccoli and potatoes dauphinois make good accompaniments.

___

400 ml/14 fl oz GAME STOCK, SEE PAGE 22

115 ml/4 fl oz MADEIRA

SPRIG OF THYME

2 SHALLOTS, CHOPPED

8 JUNIPER BERRIES, CRUSHED (SOAKED IN A LITTLE GIN, OPTIONAL)

4 PARTRIDGES, ABOUT 450 g/1 lb EACH
40 g/1½ oz UNSALTED BUTTER, DICED
SALT AND FRESHLY GROUND BLACK PEPPER
APPROX 16 SMALL GIROLLES STEAMED OVER GAME
STOCK FOR ABOUT 1 MINUTE, TO SERVE
SMALL SPRIGS OF THYME, FOR GARNISH

———————

Simmer together the stock, Madeira, thyme and shallots for 20 minutes.

Drain the juniper berries if they have been soaked in gin, then put two in the cavity of each bird.

Steam the partridges over the stock for about 20 minutes, until pink in the centre. Remove from the heat and keep warm.

Remove the thyme and shallot from the steaming liquor. Boil the liquor until slightly syrupy, adding the juices that come from the birds towards the end of the reduction. Reduce the heat to very low and gradually stir in the butter, making sure each piece is fully incorporated before adding the next. Season with salt and pepper.

To serve, remove the legs from the partridges and cut the breasts into slices. Pour the sauce on to 4 warmed plates, arrange the breasts, legs and the girolles on top, and garnish with small sprigs of thyme.

GUINEA FOWL WITH GRAPES
SERVES 4

Until recently I tended to avoid guinea fowl because their flesh lacked character but now there is a definite improvement in the flavour of some of the birds available, especially those from France or fed on maize. This recipe is equally delicious hot or cold.

700 g/1½ lb SEEDLESS WHITE GRAPES, PREFERABLY
MUSCAT, CUT INTO HALVES

150 ml/5 fl oz AQUAVIT OR GIN

1 LARGE GUINEA FOWL, APPROXIMATELY 1.5 kg/3 lb,
OR TWO SMALLER ONES

300 ml/½ PINT CHICKEN STOCK

50 ml/2 fl oz CRÈME FRAÎCHE OR DOUBLE CREAM

15 g/½ oz UNSALTED BUTTER

SEEDLESS WHITE GRAPES, FOR GARNISH

Soak the grapes in the aquavit or gin for at least 4 hours, preferably 8.

Drain the grapes, reserving the liquid. Place about a third of the grapes in the cavity of the guinea fowl then place the remainder on the bottom of a steaming basket, large colander or rack to make a bed for the bird. Place the guinea fowl on the grapes. Cover tightly. Add the reserved liquid to the stock then steam the guinea fowl over this liquid for about an hour until just cooked (if the level of stock gets too low, add a little more).

Transfer the grapes from the steaming basket, colander or rack to a blender or food processor. Pour the juices from inside the guinea fowl into the blender or food processor. Keep the guinea fowl warm or, if preferred, leave to cool and serve cold.

Purée the grapes with the steaming liquor then pass through a sieve, pressing down well on the contents of the sieve to press through as much of the juice as possible. If you do not have a blender or food processor, transfer the grapes to a sieve, press them through then mix with the steaming liquor.

Boil the grape juice until slightly syrupy and reduced to about 250 ml (9 fl oz). Lower the heat and stir in the crème fraîche or double cream. Boil again until slightly thickened, lower the heat and stir in the butter. Taste and adjust the seasoning – depending on the flavour and sweetness of the grapes it may be necessary to add a squeeze of lemon juice or a little sugar.

Remove the skin from the guinea fowl, carve the flesh, place on warmed plates, garnish with seedless white grapes and serve with the sauce.

PHEASANT WITH ELDERBERRIES

SERVES 4

Fresh elderberries and young pheasants combine beautifully in one dish. However, if using older birds the cooking time may need to be extended. When fresh elderberries are not available, use frozen elderberries or ½ tablespoon of elderberry jelly instead and sharpen the sauce with a little lemon juice.

MACE

2 HEN PHEASANTS, ABOUT 1 kg/2 lb 2 oz EACH

SALT AND FRESHLY GROUND BLACK PEPPER

HANDFUL OF ELDERBERRIES + 175 g/6 oz FOR THE SAUCE

450 ml/16 fl oz VEAL STOCK, SEE PAGE 24

75 ml/3 fl oz PORT

25 g/1 oz UNSALTED BUTTER, DICED

Rub a little mace into the skin of the pheasants. Sprinkle a little inside, then season the pheasants inside and out with salt and black pepper. Place some elderberries in the cavity of each bird. Steam the birds over the stock for about 25–30 minutes, until still slightly pink. Remove from the heat and keep warm.

Meanwhile, in a separate saucepan gently heat the elderberries for the sauce. Cover and shake the pan occasionally, until the juices begin to run. Add the port and boil until reduced to 50 ml/2 fl oz.

After steaming the pheasants, add the stock to the port mixture and boil until reduced to about 175 ml/6 fl oz, or until it coats the back of a spoon. Pass through a non-metallic sieve then reheat gently. Swirl in the butter over a very low heat, making sure each piece is fully incorporated before adding the next. Taste and adjust the seasoning and consistency if necessary.

Serve the pheasants, either carved or simply divided into halves, with the sauce poured around or over.

RABBIT WITH WALNUT SAUCE

SERVES 4

Using a mixture of game, veal or chicken stock adds character to the rabbit flesh without making it too strong. However, if you prefer a more delicate flavour, use all veal or all chicken stock. This dish can also be served cold but as it has little colour, plan an attractive garnish.

---

115 ml/4 fl oz GAME STOCK, SEE PAGE 22

175 ml/6 fl oz VEAL STOCK, SEE PAGE 24, OR CHICKEN STOCK, SEE PAGE 21

15 g/½ oz FRENCH BREAD WITHOUT CRUSTS, OR OTHER DRY BREAD

4 RABBIT PORTIONS EG SADDLES ABOUT 250 g/9 oz, HIND LEGS ABOUT 150 g/5 oz

75 g/3 oz SHELLED WALNUTS, PREFERABLY FRESH, CHOPPED

1 CLOVE OF GARLIC, CRUSHED

SALT AND FRESHLY GROUND BLACK PEPPER

APPROX 1 TEASPOON GROUND MACE

SPRIGS OF HERBS WITH FLOWERS, FOR GARNISH

Mix together the two stocks. Break the bread into pieces and soak in a little of the stock for 10 minutes.

Steam the rabbit portions over the remaining stock for about 4½–5 minutes each side (adjust the timings according to the size of portions, see page 100). Remove from the heat and keep warm.

Purée or pound in a mortar until smooth, 175 ml/6 fl oz of the stock, the soaked bread, nuts and garlic. Reheat, adding salt, pepper and ground mace to taste.

To serve, pour the sauce over the rabbit and garnish with sprigs of herbs with flowers.

HARE WITH PORT SAUCE

SERVES 4

This recipe also works well with venison. Steamed celeriac, perhaps scooped into balls with a melon baller, makes a good vegetable accompaniment.

---

4 FILLETS OF HARE

FRESHLY GROUND BLACK PEPPER

2 TABLESPOONS FINELY CRUSHED JUNIPER BERRIES

300 ml/½ PINT VEAL STOCK, SEE PAGE 24

115 ml/4 fl oz PORT

200 ml/7 fl oz FULL-BODIED RED WINE

115 g/4 oz UNSALTED BUTTER, DICED

1 TABLESPOON DIJON MUSTARD

SMALL SPRIGS OF THYME, PREFERABLY WITH FLOWERS, FOR GARNISH

Season the hare with a little freshly ground black pepper, then press the juniper berries into the flesh. Cover and leave in a cool place for 4 hours. Pour the stock, port and wine into a steamer or large pan. Steam the hare over this liquid for 3–5 minutes. Turn the fillets over half-way through so they remain pink in the centre. Remove from the heat and keep warm.

To make the sauce, boil the steaming liquor until reduced to 50 ml/2 fl oz. Lower the heat, then gradually whisk in the butter, making sure each piece is incorporated before adding the next. Finally, whisk in the mustard, to taste, and adjust the seasoning, if necessary.

To serve, cut the fillets into slices and reform their shape. Pour the sauce on to 4 warmed plates, arrange the hare on top and garnish with small sprigs of thyme.

VENISON WITH BEETROOT

SERVES 4

This colourful dish offers interesting contrasts of flavours and textures. The small amounts of crème fraîche or double cream and butter round off the sauce beautifully.

---

4 VENISON STEAKS, EACH ABOUT 150–175 g/5–6 oz AND 2.5 cm/1 in THICK

3 COOKED BEETROOT ABOUT 40 g/1½ oz EACH, THINLY SLICED

115 g/4 oz COOKED BEETROOT, CHOPPED

300 ml/½ PINT GAME STOCK, SEE PAGE 22

4 TEASPOONS CRÈME FRAÎCHE OR DOUBLE CREAM

20 g/¾ oz UNSALTED BUTTER, DICED

SALT AND FRESHLY GROUND BLACK PEPPER

Cover one side of each piece of venison with thin slices of beetroot. Use the remaining slices to make 4 circles on the bottom of a steaming basket or on a rack, to fit beneath the steaks. Place the steaks on top.

Add the chopped beetroot to the stock and steam the venison over this for about 4 minutes. Remove from the heat and keep warm.

Boil the stock with the chopped beetroot until well reduced. Purée then return to the pan and heat until all the excess liquid has evaporated. Stir in the crème fraîche or double cream and boil until slightly thickened. Reduce the heat to very low and gradually stir in the butter, making sure each piece has been incorporated before adding the next. Season with salt and pepper.

To serve, pour the sauce on to 4 warmed plates. Keeping the beetroot slices on top and beneath, place the venison on the sauce.

MEAT

Although the better cuts of meat are best suited to steaming, other less tender cuts can be used if marinated in something acidic, such as wine or yoghurt, or beaten beforehand to soften the fibres. Alternatively the meat can be tenderized by slowing down the rate of cooking; this is done by lining the steaming basket with foil or placing the meat in a dish.

The length of cooking is affected by the quality of each particular piece of meat, the cut, thickness, initial temperature (I always use meat that is at a cool room temperature, not straight from the freezer) and the actual joint, which can be affected by how the animal was slaughtered and the length of time it was hung.

The shorter the time allowed for cooking the more important these factors become. Also bear in mind that if you are using the steaming liquor to make a sauce you will need to allow the time that this will take after the meat has been cooked.

The times in the recipes and chart are for meat that is rare or pink; even the pork is cooked surprisingly lightly because modern methods of rearing, slaughtering and refrigeration eliminate the need for the pork to be well-cooked or overcooked, which is more often the case. If in doubt about steaming the meat, err on the side of undercooking, as it only takes a couple of minutes to increase the degree of 'doneness'.

The times given in the recipes and chart include 'resting' time before serving. During this period, the heat and juices become evenly distributed throughout the meat. The flesh settles and it cooks a little further. To test the meat after resting, press gently with the back of a spoon. If it springs back, it will be cooked lightly. If you make a cut to test before giving it time to rest it will appear more bloody and underdone than it actually is. Cutting also allows the juices to escape.

Meat	Weight	Steaming time
Beef		
Fillet steak	150 g / 5 oz	2–3 mins a side
Rump steak	225 g / 8 oz	5 mins a side
	150 g / 5 oz	2–3 mins a side
Gammon		
Steak	150 g / 5 oz	4–5 mins a side
Lamb		
Steaks	175 g / 6 oz	4 mins a side
Boneless chop	150 g / 5 oz	3 mins a side
Boneless loin, skinned	350 g / 12 oz	12–14 mins
Boneless rack (best end)	350 g / 12 oz	12–14 mins
Noisettes		3 mins a side
Offal		
Kidneys, halved	45 g / 1¾ oz	1½ mins a side
Sweetbreads	1.5 cm / ½ in slices	4–5 mins
Pork		
Boneless chop	200 g / 7 oz	4–5 mins a side
Boneless steak	175 g / 6 oz	3½–4 mins a side
Cubes		4 mins
Strips		3 mins
Veal		
Escalope		2 mins a side
Shoulder, cubed		6 mins

STUFFED LEEKS

SERVES 4

Eight fat, slit leek leaf 'tubes' are needed for this recipe so if you are unable to get one nice, fat leek you will need to use the outer leaves of two slimmer ones.

---

2 TABLESPOONS BURGHUL

1 FIRM FAT LEEK, WHITE PART ABOUT 10 cm/4 in LONG WHEN TRIMMED

225 g/8 oz MINCED LEAN BEEF

10 DRIED APRICOTS, CHOPPED, SOAKED AND DRAINED

2½ TABLESPOONS FINELY CHOPPED PARSLEY

1 TABLESPOON CHOPPED MINT

SALT AND FRESHLY GROUND BLACK PEPPER

1 SMALL CARROT, THICKLY SLICED

BOUQUET GARNI OF A BAY LEAF, SPRIG OF PARSLEY AND SPRIG OF THYME

450 ml/16 fl oz BROWN VEAL STOCK, SEE PAGE 25

Pour 75 ml/3 fl oz hot water over the burghul and leave to soak for 20 minutes.

Meanwhile, cut through the leek, lengthways, as far as the centre then carefully separate enough individual leaves to give 8 slit tubes. Discard the outer ones if they are papery. Take the inner leaves of the leek and chop enough to make 3 tablespoons.

Drain the burghul, squeeze out excess moisture, then mix with the beef, chopped leeks, apricots and herbs. Season with salt and pepper. Spoon the mixture into the leaves to give 8 filled tubes. Add the carrot and bouquet garni to the stock then steam the leeks, seam-side uppermost, over this liquid for about 18 minutes. Remove from the heat and keep the leeks warm.

Boil the steaming liquor until reduced to about 175 ml/6 fl oz.
Remove the carrots and herbs, taste and adjust the seasoning.
Serve the leeks with the reduced liquor poured over.

FINGERS OF BEEF IN A RICH BROWN SAUCE

SERVES 4

Marinating the fibres of less prime, but tasty, cuts of beef, makes it
more tender. Good accompanying vegetables for this richly
flavoured dish are mushrooms and broccoli.

---

625 g/1 lb 6 oz TOP SIDE OR BLADE STEAK, ABOUT
2.5 cm/1 in THICK, CUT INTO 4 PIECES AND
WELL TRIMMED

3 SHALLOTS, FINELY CHOPPED

450 ml/16 fl oz BROWN VEAL STOCK, SEE PAGE 25

1 SMALL SPRIG OF TARRAGON

2 TEASPOONS MOUTARDE DE MEAUX

SQUEEZE OF LEMON JUICE

15 g/½ oz UNSALTED BUTTER, DICED

TARRAGON AND DICED TOMATO FLESH OR DICED
CARROTS, FOR GARNISH

MARINADE

400 ml/14 fl oz RED WINE

1 SMALL ONION, CHOPPED

1 CARROT, CHOPPED

1 BAY LEAF, BROKEN

4 JUNIPER BERRIES, CRUSHED

SALT AND FRESHLY GROUND BLACK PEPPER

Mix together all the ingredients for the marinade. Place the beef in a shallow, non-metallic dish, pour the marinade over, cover and leave in a cool place for 6–8 hours, turning the meat occasionally.

Lift out the meat, allow the excess marinade to drain off, then pat dry. Strain the marinade, then boil until the liquid is reduced to 50 ml/2 fl oz. Remove the bay leaf.

Add the shallots to the stock then steam the beef over the stock for about 17 minutes. Remove from the heat and keep warm.

Add the tarragon and reduced marinade to the stock and boil until reduced to 225 ml/8 fl oz. Remove the tarragon. Purée the reduced stock with the mustard to a slightly coarse texture. Reheat gently. Add a squeeze of lemon juice and finish by swirling in the butter, making sure each piece is incorporated before adding the next. Taste and adjust the consistency, flavourings and seasoning, if necessary.

Cut the beef into approximately 2.5 cm/1 in cubes and add to the sauce.

To serve, garnish with a scattering of tarragon leaves and diced tomato or carrots.

STEAK WITH HORSERADISH AND TURNIP SHREDS

SERVES 4

4 RUMP STEAKS, ABOUT 115 g/4 oz EACH
2 TABLESPOONS HORSERADISH RELISH
450 ml/16 fl oz BROWN VEAL STOCK, SEE PAGE 25
200 g/7 oz YOUNG TURNIPS, GRATED
FRESHLY GROUND WHITE PEPPER

Using the point of a small sharp knife, cut a deep pocket in each steak. Spread about ½ teaspoon of the horseradish relish on both sides of each steak, then spread about 1 teaspoonful in each pocket. Leave in a cool place for about 2 hours.

Steam the steaks over the stock for 2 minutes each side. Remove the steaks and keep warm. Steam the turnips in a shallow layer over the stock for about 2 minutes. Season with white pepper and keep warm with the steaks. Boil the stock until reduced to 200 ml/7 fl oz. Taste and adjust the seasoning.

Serve the steaks and turnips with the sauce poured around.

STEAK, KIDNEY AND OYSTER PUDDING
SERVES 4–6

Cooking the beef beforehand improves the final taste of the pudding, as the flavours of the filling will have had a chance to mingle and mature during their overnight standing. It also allows the fat that comes out of the meat during cooking to be removed before the pudding is assembled. The use of oysters dates from Mrs Beeton's day, when they were cheap. Nowadays, native oysters are really out of the question for this type of dish, but Pacific or Portuguese oysters, which are much cheaper, could be used. Alternatively, use additional mushrooms.

---

25 g/1 oz BEEF DRIPPING OR BUTTER

1 ONION, CHOPPED

675 g/1½ lb STEWING STEAK, WELL TRIMMED AND CUT INTO 2.5 cm/1 in CUBES

2 TABLESPOONS SEASONED FLOUR

150 g/5 oz LAMBS' KIDNEYS, TRIMMED AND CUT INTO 2.5 cm/1 in CUBES

115 g/4 oz MUSHROOMS

200 ml/7 fl oz BROWN VEAL STOCK, SEE PAGE 25

225 ml/8 fl oz FULL-BODIED RED WINE

BOUQUET GARNI OF 1 BAY LEAF, 6 PARSLEY STALKS
AND SPRIG OF THYME
SALT AND FRESHLY GROUND BLACK PEPPER
12 OYSTERS

PASTRY
225 g/8 oz SELF-RAISING FLOUR
1 TABLESPOON BAKING POWDER
1 TEASPOON FINELY GRATED LEMON RIND
1 TABLESPOON FINELY CHOPPED PARSLEY
75 g/3 oz SHREDDED BEEF SUET
50 g/2 oz HARD, UNSALTED BUTTER, FINELY DICED
1 EGG, BEATEN

Melt half of the dripping or butter in a large pan, add the onion and
cook, stirring occasionally, for 2–3 minutes. Coat the steak in the
seasoned flour, add to the pan and cook, stirring frequently, until
lightly browned. Remove with a slotted spoon and place in a heavy-
based casserole. Coat the kidney in seasoned flour, stir into the pan
and cook, turning occasionally, for 2–3 minutes. Transfer to the
casserole using a slotted spoon. Melt the remaining dripping in the
pan, add the mushrooms and cook, stirring occasionally, for 2–3
minutes. Transfer to the casserole using a slotted spoon.

Stir the stock and wine into the pan, dislodging the sediment, and
bring to the boil. Add the bouquet garni and seasoning, pour into the
casserole, cover tightly and cook in a preheated oven 180°C/350°F
(gas mark 4) for 1½–2 hours. Remove from the oven, uncover and stir
occasionally to hasten the cooling. When cold, cover and keep in a
cold place overnight.

On the day the pudding is required, mix together the flour, baking
powder, lemon rind and parsley. Stir in the suet and butter, then add
the egg and sufficient cold water to bind the ingredients to a soft,
pliable dough. On a lightly floured surface knead lightly and, using a
floured rolling pin, roll out three-quarters of the dough to a large

circle and use to line a 900 ml / 1½ pint pudding basin. Press it in lightly. Roll out the remaining portion to make a lid.

Remove the fat from the surface of the meat and lift out and discard the bouquet garni. If there is an excessive amount of liquid, especially if oysters are used, pour it out and boil until reduced, then return it to the meat. Add the oysters and their liquid, if used, to the meat and check the seasoning. Spoon into the lined pudding basin, dampen the edge of the lining pastry then cover with the lid and seal the edges firmly together. Cover the top with a circle of greaseproof paper, then a piece of foil pleated across the centre and secure in place with string. Steam for 1½–2 hours.

Serve the pudding in its basin with a white napkin tied around it.

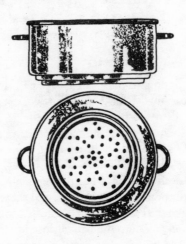

STEAK MARINATED IN MANDARIN

SERVES 4

2 TABLESPOONS ORANGE OR MANDARIN
MARMALADE
1 TEASPOON FINELY CHOPPED FRESH ROOT GINGER
1 CLOVE OF GARLIC, CHOPPED
SALT AND COARSELY GROUND WHITE PEPPER
50 ml/2 fl oz LEMON JUICE
50 ml/2 fl oz ORANGE JUICE
50 ml/2 fl oz WHITE WINE VINEGAR
115 ml/4 fl oz OLIVE OIL
2 × 225 g/8 oz FILLET STEAKS
BROWN VEAL STOCK FOR STEAMING, SEE PAGE 25
MIXED SALAD LEAVES – RADICCHIO, CORN SALAD,
CURLY ENDIVE, CHICORY

GINGER VINAIGRETTE

1 SHALLOT, FINELY CHOPPED
1.25 cm/½ in PIECE FRESH ROOT GINGER, PEELED AND
FINELY CHOPPED
50 ml/2 fl oz OLIVE OIL
115 ml/4 fl oz RICE WINE VINEGAR
1 TABLESPOON DARK SESAME OIL
SALT AND FRESHLY GROUND PEPPER, PREFERABLY
WHITE AND BLACK MIXED

Simmer together the marmalade, ginger, garlic, salt and pepper, fruit juices and vinegar until reduced to 115 ml/4 fl oz. Leave to cool, then stir in the olive oil.

Meanwhile, mix together the ingredients for the ginger vinaigrette.

Brush the steaks with some of the reduced mixture and leave to marinate in a non-metallic dish for up to 4 hours.

Steam the steaks over the stock for about 5 minutes each side, depending on the degree to which you like them cooked. Remove from the heat and leave the steaks to rest for about 5 minutes in a warm place.

While you are waiting, toss the salad with the ginger vinaigrette and divide between 4 plates.

Cut each steak into diagonal slices and serve with the dressed salad.

STEAKS WITH CHINESE MUSHROOM SAUCE

SERVES 4

---

1 LARGE CLOVE OF GARLIC, CHOPPED

1 SHALLOT, CHOPPED

1 CARROT, QUARTERED

1 LITRE/1¾ PINTS BROWN VEAL STOCK, SEE PAGE 25

50 g/2 oz DRIED CHINESE MUSHROOMS, SOAKED IN BOILING WATER FOR 30 MINUTES

4 FILLET STEAKS, ABOUT 150 g/5 oz EACH

115 g/4 oz UNSALTED BUTTER, DICED

WILD MUSHROOMS, OYSTER MUSHROOMS OR BUTTON MUSHROOMS, FINELY CHOPPED

FINELY CHOPPED PARSLEY, FOR GARNISH

Simmer the garlic, shallot and carrot in the stock for 20 minutes.

In the meantime, remove the Chinese mushrooms from the soaking water. Strain the water and reserve. Chop these mushrooms and add to the stock with the reserved water. Simmer for 30 minutes then steam the steaks over the stock for 2–3 minutes each side, depending on the degree to which you like them cooked. Remove from the heat and keep warm.

Strain the stock through a sieve, pushing down well. Boil the strained liquid until reduced to 50 ml/2 fl oz. Lower the heat so the liquid is just below simmering point, then gradually whisk in the butter, making sure each piece is fully incorporated before adding the next.

Steam the mushrooms for the garnish (see page 174).

To serve, pour the sauce around the steaks and garnish with the mushrooms and parsley.

STEAKS WITH SHALLOTS

SERVES 4

If preferred, entrecôte or rump steaks can be used instead of fillet steaks. See page 138 for cooking times.

---

3 SHALLOTS, FINELY CHOPPED
1 SMALL SPRIG OF THYME
2 SPRIGS OF LOVAGE
400 ml/14 fl oz BROWN VEAL STOCK, SEE PAGE 25
4 FILLET STEAKS, ABOUT 150 g/5 oz EACH
2 TOMATOES, SKINNED AND SEEDS REMOVED, COARSELY CHOPPED
25 g/1 oz UNSALTED BUTTER, DICED
SALT AND FRESHLY GROUND BLACK PEPPER
SQUEEZE OF LEMON JUICE
LOVAGE LEAVES, FOR GARNISH

Simmer the shallots and herbs in the stock for 20 minutes. Then, in a steaming basket or colander, steam the steaks over this liquid for 2–3 minutes each side, adding the tomatoes for the last 1½ minutes or so.

Remove the basket or colander from the pan and keep the steaks and tomatoes warm.

Boil the stock until reduced to 150 ml / ¼ pint. Remove the herbs, lower the heat and swirl in the butter, making sure each piece is incorporated before adding the next. Season with salt and pepper, and add a small squeeze of lemon juice.

To serve, pour the sauce over the steaks, top with the tomatoes and garnish with lovage leaves.

VEAL FRICASSEE
SERVES 4

---

450 g/1 lb SHOULDER OF VEAL, CUBED
2 BAY LEAVES
2 LARGE SPRIGS OF PARSLEY
2 SPRIGS OF MARJORAM
200 ml/7 fl oz MEDIUM-BODIED DRY WHITE WINE
3 TABLESPOONS LEMON JUICE
4 PEARL ONIONS, HALVED
1 CARROT, CHOPPED
1 LEEK, SLICED
1 CLOVE OF GARLIC, COARSELY CHOPPED
450 ml/16 fl oz VEAL STOCK, SEE PAGE 24
115 g/4 oz FROMAGE BLANC
CHOPPED THYME, FOR GARNISH
STEAMED BROCCOLI FLORETS, BABY OR
QUARTERED CARROTS AND PEARL ONIONS
TO SERVE

Place the cubes of veal in a shallow, non-metallic dish with one bay leaf, a sprig of parsley and a sprig of marjoram. Pour over the wine and lemon juice. Cover and leave to marinate for 12 hours, gently stirring the ingredients around occasionally.

Lift out the veal, drain off and reserve the marinade. Add the onions, carrot, leek, garlic, reserved marinade and remaining herbs to the stock and steam the veal over this liquid for 6 minutes. Remove from the heat and keep warm.

Boil the steaming liquor until reduced to 115 ml/4 fl oz. Pass through a sieve and reheat. Over a low heat, stir in the fromage blanc and heat through gently. Carefully stir in the veal.

Transfer the veal to a warmed serving dish, pour the sauce over, sprinkle with thyme and place the broccoli florets, carrots and pearl onions around.

VEAL WRAPPED WITH A PARMA HAM JACKET

SERVES 4

Turkey escalopes can also be served in this way.

---

4 ESCALOPES OF VEAL
SALT AND FRESHLY GROUND BLACK PEPPER
4 LARGE SLICES OF PARMA HAM
2 TABLESPOONS FINELY CHOPPED BASIL
300 ml/½ PINT VEAL STOCK, SEE PAGE 24
150 ml/¼ PINT MEDIUM-BODIED DRY WHITE WINE
175 g/6 oz UNSALTED BUTTER, DICED
LEMON JUICE
BASIL LEAVES, FOR GARNISH

Sandwich each piece of veal between two sheets of greaseproof paper and beat out. Season the veal with black pepper, then place each escalope on a slice of ham. Sprinkle the basil along the centre of each piece of veal. Roll up the ham, enclosing the escalopes and keeping the line of basil in the centre. Secure with wooden cocktail sticks.

Boil the stock and wine together for 10 minutes then, in a steaming basket or colander, steam the rolls over the liquid for about 7–8 minutes. Remove the basket or colander from the pan and keep the veal rolls warm.

Boil the steaming liquid until reduced to 50 ml/2 fl oz. Lower the heat and gradually whisk in the butter, making sure each piece is incorporated before adding the next. Season with salt, pepper and a little lemon juice.

Remove the cocktail sticks from the veal rolls and cut into slices using a sharp knife. To serve, pour the sauce on to 4 warmed plates, place the veal slices on top and garnish with basil leaves.

LIGHT BALLS OF VEAL
IN LETTUCE CUPS

SERVES 4

---

450 g/1 lb LEAN VEAL, MINCED
50 g/2 oz SOFT CHEESE
1 SMALL EGG WHITE
SALT AND FRESHLY GROUND BLACK PEPPER
½ SMALL RED PEPPER, FINELY CHOPPED
½ SMALL YELLOW PEPPER, FINELY CHOPPED
½ SMALL GREEN PEPPER, FINELY CHOPPED
400 ml/14 fl oz VEAL STOCK, SEE PAGE 24
1 EGG YOLK
2 TABLESPOONS LEMON JUICE
APPROX 2 TABLESPOONS CHOPPED CHERVIL
FRESHLY GROUND WHITE PEPPER
APPROX 40 g/1½ oz SHREDDED LETTUCE
4 ICEBERG LETTUCE LEAVES THAT FORM
NATURAL 'CUPS'
STRIPS OF BLANCHED RED PEPPER, FOR GARNISH

Gently but thoroughly mix together the veal, cheese, beaten egg white, salt and black pepper. Form carefully into 12 balls. Cover and chill for at least an hour.

Mix together the peppers and season lightly. Steam the peppers and veal balls over the stock for 2–3 minutes. Remove from the heat and keep warm.

Boil the stock until reduced to 225 ml/8 fl oz. In a separate bowl, mix the egg yolk with the lemon juice, add the chervil, then whisk in a little of the stock. Reduce the heat below the stock to very low and gradually whisk in the egg yolk mixture. Continue to whisk until the sauce thickens slightly. Remove from the heat, season with freshly ground white pepper and adjust the levels of lemon juice and chervil, if necessary.

Divide the shredded lettuce and peppers between the lettuce cups and place the veal balls on top. Fold the lettuce leaves over and criss-cross the blanched strips of red pepper to resemble string. Serve the sauce separately, to pour into the parcels.

VEAL CHOPS WITH MARJORAM AND LEMON

SERVES 4

A traditional Italian dish, but steamed rather than cooked in oil. As an alternative to veal, use pork chops, trimmed of all fat, instead but increase the cooking time by about 30–60 seconds each side.

---

4 VEAL CHOPS, ABOUT 200 g/7 oz EACH AND 2.5 cm/1 in THICK

14 SPRIGS OF MARJORAM

1–2 CLOVES OF GARLIC (OPTIONAL)

4 TABLESPOONS LEMON JUICE

VEAL STOCK FOR STEAMING (OPTIONAL), SEE PAGE 24

SMALL SPRIGS OF MARJORAM AND SLICES OF LEMON, FOR GARNISH

Cut a slit in the side of each veal chop to make a pocket. Insert into each a sprig of marjoram. If using garlic, crush it with the lemon juice. Sprinkle a little of this mixture, or just lemon juice, into each pocket and rub some on the outside of each chop.

Make a bed of some of the marjoram sprigs in the bottom of a steaming basket or colander, place the chops on the sprigs and sprinkle more marjoram sprigs on top. Cover and leave in a cool place for about 30 minutes.

Steam the veal over the stock, or seasoned water, for about 3½ minutes each side, until lightly cooked.

To serve, remove the marjoram sprigs and pour any remaining lemon juice and garlic over the veal. Garnish with small sprigs of marjoram and slices of lemon.

LAMB WITH TOMATOES, MUSHROOMS AND BASIL

SERVES 4

115 g/4 oz MUSHROOMS, CHOPPED

SALT AND FRESHLY GROUND BLACK PEPPER

4 LAMB STEAKS, ABOUT 175 g/6 oz EACH

4 MEDITERRANEAN TOMATOES, SKINNED AND
SEEDS REMOVED, FINELY CHOPPED

2 TABLESPOONS CHOPPED BASIL

200 ml/7 fl oz MEDIUM-BODIED DRY WHITE WINE

SPRIG OF ROSEMARY

200 ml/7 fl oz VEAL STOCK, SEE PAGE 24

50 g/2 oz UNSALTED BUTTER, DICED

SMALL BASIL LEAVES, FOR GARNISH

Sprinkle the mushrooms with a little salt and pepper, then pack into 4 'cake' shapes and place in a steaming basket or colander. Place a lamb steak on top of each 'cake' of mushrooms.

Mix together the tomatoes and basil, season lightly and place on the lamb. Add the wine and rosemary to the stock and steam the lamb over this liquid for about 8 minutes, depending on the thickness of the meat, until pink in the centre. Remove from the heat and keep warm.

Take the rosemary out of the steaming liquor, then boil until it is reduced to 150 ml/¼ pint. Lower the heat and gradually whisk in the butter, making sure each piece is incorporated before adding the next. Taste and adjust the seasoning.

To serve, use a fish slice to transfer the lamb, with the mushrooms beneath and the tomatoes above, to 4 warmed plates. Pour the sauce around and garnish the tomatoes with small basil leaves.

LAMB WITH TARRAGON

SERVES 4

8 SPRIGS OF TARRAGON
4 NOISETTES OF LAMB
1 SMALL SHALLOT, FINELY CHOPPED
115 ml/4 fl oz DRY WHITE VERMOUTH
300 ml/½ PINT VEAL STOCK, SEE PAGE 24
2 TEASPOONS FINELY CHOPPED TARRAGON
115 ml/4 fl oz DOUBLE CREAM
15 g/½ oz UNSALTED BUTTER, DICED
SALT AND FRESHLY GROUND BLACK PEPPER
SPRIGS OF TARRAGON, FOR GARNISH

Put 4 sprigs of tarragon in the bottom of a steaming basket or large colander. Lay a noisette on top of each sprig and place the remaining sprigs on top. In a small saucepan simmer the shallot in the vermouth until nearly all the liquid has evaporated. Stir in a little of the stock, then pour this liquid into a steamer or large saucepan containing the remaining stock. Steam the noisettes over this liquid for about 3 minutes each side, so they are pink in the centre. Remove from the heat and keep warm.

Boil the steaming liquor until reduced to 115 ml/4 fl oz. Stir in the tarragon and cream and simmer until the sauce begins to thicken. Lower the heat and gradually stir in the butter, making sure each piece is incorporated before adding the next. Season with salt and pepper to taste.

To serve, pour the sauce on to 4 warmed plates, place the noisettes on top and garnish with sprigs of tarragon.

LAMB WITH ROSEMARY AND THYME SAUCE

SERVES 4

---

2 SMALL SHALLOTS, FINELY CHOPPED
300 ml/½ PINT FULL-BODIED DRY WHITE WINE
SMALL SPRIG OF ROSEMARY
SMALL SPRIG OF THYME
425 ml/¾ PINT VEAL STOCK, SEE PAGE 24
½ A FIRM TOMATO, DICED
2 BONED BEST ENDS OF NECK OF YOUNG LAMB,
ABOUT 350 g/12 oz EACH
FRESHLY GROUND BLACK PEPPER
15 g/½ oz UNSALTED BUTTER, DICED
SMALL SPRIGS OF ROSEMARY AND THYME, FOR
GARNISH

Simmer the shallots in the wine for about 10 minutes and the herbs in the stock. When the shallots have become soft, boil the wine until almost completely evaporated. Stir in the stock and herbs and add the tomato.

Season the lamb lightly with freshly ground black pepper and steam over the flavoured stock for about 5 minutes each side, until pink in the centre. Remove from the heat and keep warm.

To make the sauce, boil the stock until reduced to 225 ml/8 fl oz. Pass through a sieve and reheat. Over a very low heat, swirl in the butter, making sure each piece is incorporated before adding the next. Taste and season, if necessary. Keep warm but do not allow to boil.

To serve, cut the lamb into 12 or 16 slices and arrange on 4 warmed plates. Pour the sauce around and garnish with sprigs of rosemary and thyme.

LAMB WITH GREEN MUSTARD COATING

SERVES 4

---

4 TEASPOONS GREEN PEPPERCORNS, FINELY
CHOPPED

3½ TABLESPOONS CHOPPED SPRING ONIONS (GREEN
AND WHITE PARTS)

3½ TABLESPOONS WHOLE GRAIN MUSTARD

PINCH OF CAYENNE PEPPER

4 LAMB CHOPS, OR STEAKS, TRIMMED

VEAL STOCK FOR STEAMING (OPTIONAL), SEE
PAGE 24

Mix together thoroughly the peppercorns, spring onions, mustard and cayenne pepper. Spread this mixture firmly over the lamb, cover and leave for up to 12 hours in a cool place.

Steam the lamb over the stock, or seasoned water, for 3–4 minutes each side. Remove from the basket or colander, together with any of the mustard coating that may remain, and serve.

LAMB PATTIES
SERVES 4

The Aubergine Sauce (see page 104), minus the coriander, goes well with these patties.

———

400 g/14 oz LEAN, YOUNG LAMB, FINELY MINCED AND CHILLED

50 g/2 oz LIGHTLY SMOKED, DERINDED BACON, FINELY CHOPPED AND CHILLED

40 g/1½ oz PINE NUTS

1 TEASPOON FRESHLY GROUND CORIANDER

SALT AND COARSELY GROUND BLACK PEPPER

LAMB STOCK FOR STEAMING (OPTIONAL), SEE PAGE 23

CORIANDER SPRIGS, FOR GARNISH

———

Mix together all the ingredients except the steaming liquid and coriander sprigs. Then, lightly but firmly, form into 8 patties, about 2.5 cm/1 in thick.

Steam the patties over the stock, or seasoned water, for 2–3 minutes each side.

To serve, sprinkle each patty with coriander sprigs.

LAMB WITH YOGHURT AND MINT

SERVES 4

---

300 ml/½ PINT THICK PLAIN YOGHURT
1 SMALL ONION, FINELY CHOPPED
2 TABLESPOONS FINELY CHOPPED MINT
1 TABLESPOON OLIVE OIL
1 TABLESPOON LIME OR LEMON JUICE
SALT AND FRESHLY GROUND WHITE PEPPER
4 BONELESS LAMB STEAKS, ABOUT 175 g/6 oz EACH
4 MINT LEAVES
SMALL SPRIGS OF MINT, FOR GARNISH

Beat the yoghurt until smooth then mix in the onion, mint, oil, lime or lemon juice. Season with salt and pepper, then spread this mixture over both sides of the lamb. Place in a non-metallic dish, cover and leave in a cool place for 4–8 hours, turning the meat over occasionally.

Remove the lamb from the marinade, place a mint leaf on top of each steak and steam for about 4 minutes each side. Lift the mint leaves from the lamb when turning the steaks and replace on the upper side. Serve the lamb garnished with small sprigs of mint.

LAMB THREADED WITH LEMON

SERVES 4

If you do not have any ready-made veal stock, use chicken stock or
seasoned water flavoured with lots of herbs.
For an enriched sauce simmer 2 chopped shallots in 50 ml/2 fl oz
dry white vermouth until the liquid has almost evaporated
completely. Then stir in the lemon juice from the marinade and add
this mixture to the stock.

---

2 LEMONS

2 BONED AND SKINNED LOINS OF LAMB, ABOUT
400 g/14 oz EACH

300 ml/½ PINT VEAL STOCK, SEE PAGE 24

SALT AND FRESHLY GROUND BLACK PEPPER

SPRIGS OF PARSLEY, FOR GARNISH

Peel the lemons thinly with a vegetable peeler, keeping the rind in
long strips. Cut the strips lengthways into even finer strips. Open out
the loins of lamb and lay strips of lemon rind along the natural
openings; ease out as much of the muscle as will come and insert strips
of lemon peel. Then, using the point of a fine, sharp knife, make
incisions into the loins from the skinned side and insert more strips of
lemon peel. Reserve the strips of peel left over.

Place the loins in a shallow, non-metallic dish. Squeeze the lemons
and pour the juice over the lamb. Cover and leave for 2 hours, turning
the lamb occasionally.

Pour the marinade into the stock and steam the lamb, skinned side
uppermost first, over the stock for 6 minutes each side, until pink in
the centre. Remove from the heat and keep warm.

Boil the stock until slightly syrupy and reduced to about 150 ml/¼
pint. Stir in the reserved strips of lemon peel and season with salt and
pepper, if necessary. Keep warm.

To serve, carve the lamb into slices and pour the sauce over. Garnish with sprigs of parsley.

PORK WITH
WATERCRESS SAUCE

SERVES 4

---

175 g/6 oz WATERCRESS, WELL TRIMMED, STALKS RETAINED

575 g/1¼ lb PORK TENDERLOIN, CUT INTO STRIPS ABOUT 1.25 × 6.25 cm/½ × 2½ in LONG

300 ml/½ PINT VEAL STOCK, SEE PAGE 24

1 SHALLOT, FINELY CHOPPED

3 TABLESPOONS MEDIUM-BODIED DRY WHITE WINE

175 ml/6 fl oz WHIPPING CREAM OR STRAINED GREEK YOGHURT

SALT AND FRESHLY GROUND BLACK PEPPER

WATERCRESS LEAVES, FOR GARNISH

Line the bottom of a steaming basket or colander with half of the watercress. Lay the pork on top, then cover with the remaining watercress. Add the watercress stalks to the stock, then steam the pork over this liquid for about 3 minutes. Remove the basket or colander from the heat and keep warm.

Meanwhile, in a separate pan, simmer the shallot in the wine until softened and the wine almost completely evaporated.

Boil hard the cooking liquid over which the pork was steamed until reduced to 40 ml/1½ fl oz. Strain and stir into the pan of shallot. Remove the watercress from the steaming basket and purée with the shallot and stock mixture. Stir in the cream or yoghurt and purée again. Season to taste. Warm through gently, stirring, but do not allow to boil.

To serve, pour the sauce on to 4 warmed plates, place the pork on top and garnish with watercress leaves.

COLLOPS OF PORK WITH PICKLED WALNUTS

SERVES 4

As an alternative to pork, use turkey or chicken breast, and reduce the cooking time to 5 minutes.

---

1 SLIM LEEK, CUT INTO FINE STRIPS

SALT AND FRESHLY GROUND BLACK PEPPER

450–575 g/1–1¼ lb PORK TENDERLOIN, CUT ACROSS THE GRAIN INTO SLICES ABOUT 3 mm/⅛ in THICK

12 PICKLED WALNUTS, ROUGHLY CHOPPED

115 g/4 oz ONIONS, FINELY CHOPPED

75 ml/3 fl oz MADEIRA

225 ml/8 fl oz BROWN VEAL STOCK, SEE PAGE 25

15 g/½ oz UNSALTED BUTTER, DICED

1 SPRING ONION, WHITE AND GREEN PART, FINELY CHOPPED, FOR GARNISH

Scatter the leek strips over the base of a heatproof, shallow dish. Season lightly, lay the pork on top and cover with the walnuts and onions. Sprinkle over the Madeira and 75 ml/3 fl oz of the stock.

Cover and steam for about 6–7 minutes. Remove the dish from the heat and pour off the liquid into the stock. Keep the pork and leeks warm.

Boil the stock until reduced to 150 ml/¼ pint. Lower the heat and swirl in the butter, making sure each piece is incorporated before adding the next. Season to taste.

To serve, pour the sauce over the meat, scatter the chopped spring onion over the top, and serve immediately.

PORK WITH FENNEL
SERVES 4

---

4 BONELESS PORK STEAKS OR CUTLETS, ABOUT
150 g/5 oz EACH
FRESHLY GROUND BLACK PEPPER
1 MEDIUM-SIZED FLORENCE FENNEL BULB
350 ml/12 fl oz VEAL STOCK, SEE PAGE 24, OR WATER
1 EGG YOLK
1 TABLESPOON LEMON JUICE
15 g/½ oz UNSALTED BUTTER, DICED
SPRIGS OF FENNEL, FOR GARNISH

Using a small sharp knife, make a deep incision in the side of each piece of pork to form a pocket. Season inside the pocket with freshly ground black pepper.

Remove 2 or 3 of the outer layers from the fennel, leaving about 115 g/4 oz. Cut in half, then simmer in the stock or water for 5 minutes. Remove and chop, then divide the pieces between the pockets in the pork.

Chop the outside leaves of the fennel, add to the stock or water then steam the pork over this liquid for 9–10 minutes. Remove from the heat and keep warm.

If necessary, boil the steaming liquid until reduced to 175 ml/6 fl oz. Purée with the fennel, then mix a little of the purée into the egg yolk. Pour into a small saucepan, stir in the remaining purée and heat very gently, stirring constantly, until the sauce thickens. Do not allow it to boil. Stir in the lemon juice. Whisk in the butter, making sure each piece is incorporated before adding the next. Season with pepper to taste.

Serve the pork with the sauce and garnish with sprigs of fennel.

AROMATIC LEMON PORK

SERVES 4

Use freshly ground spices for the best results.

___

450 g/1 lb PORK TENDERLOIN, CUT INTO
1.25 cm/½ in SLICES
GRATED RIND AND JUICE OF 1 LARGE LEMON
CRUSHED SEEDS FROM 6 GREEN CARDAMOM PODS
1½ TEASPOONS GROUND CORIANDER
1½ TEASPOONS GROUND CUMIN
SALT AND FRESHLY GROUND BLACK PEPPER
1 SMALL CLOVE OF GARLIC, CRUSHED
1 SMALL ONION, FINELY CHOPPED
300 ml/½ PINT VEAL STOCK, SEE PAGE 24
2 TABLESPOONS SINGLE CREAM

___

Sandwich each slice of pork between two sheets of greaseproof paper or clingfilm and beat them out. Place in a shallow non-metallic dish. Mix together the lemon rind and juice, spices, salt, pepper and garlic, and pour over the pork. Cover and leave in a cool place for 24 hours, turning the slices over occasionally.

Pack the pork into a heatproof bowl. Pour the marinating liquor into a saucepan, add the onion and stock, bring to the boil and pour over the pork. Cover the bowl tightly, place in a steaming basket or colander or on a rack and steam for 45 minutes, until the pork is tender.

Pour the cooking juices out of the bowl into a clean saucepan. Boil until slightly thickened. Lower the heat and stir in the cream. Taste and adjust the seasoning. To serve, pour the sauce back over the pork.

PORK AND ORANGE PUDDING

SERVES 4

---

50 g/2 oz DRIED APRICOTS, CHOPPED AND SOAKED OVERNIGHT

50 g/2 oz DERINDED LEAN BACON, CHOPPED

1 ONION, FINELY CHOPPED

450 g/1 lb LEAN PORK, CUBED

50 g/2 oz MUSHROOMS, SLICED

50 g/2 oz LAMBS' KIDNEY, CORE REMOVED, FINELY CHOPPED

FINELY GRATED RIND OF 1 SMALL ORANGE

2 TABLESPOONS SWEET MADEIRA OR SWEET SHERRY

FRESHLY GROUND BLACK PEPPER

PASTRY

150 g/5 oz PLAIN FLOUR

65 g/2½ oz SHREDDED SUET

1½ TEASPOONS FINELY CRUSHED SEEDS FROM CARDAMOM PODS

MILK TO MIX

Drain the apricots and reserve 4 tablespoons of the liquor.

In a nonstick pan over a low heat, gently cook the bacon until the fat begins to run. Add the onion, cover and cook gently, shaking the pan from time to time. Mix in the pork and mushrooms and cook, uncovered, stirring occasionally, for 2–3 minutes. Cook the kidney in this mixture for about a minute, then stir in the apricots, reserved soaking liquor and orange rind. Remove from the heat and pour in the Madeira or sherry. Season with black pepper and leave to cool.

To make the pastry, mix together the flour, suet and cardamom seeds and add sufficient milk to bind to a smooth, soft but not sticky, dough. Transfer the dough to a lightly floured work surface. Divide off one quarter and reserve. Roll the larger portion out to a circle large enough to line a 900 ml/1½ pint pudding basin. Line the basin with the dough then roll out the reserved dough to make a circle to cover the top.

Fill the basin with the pork mixture then cover with the dough lid, pressing the edges of the lid and the lining dough firmly together. Cover the pudding with a circle of greaseproof paper, then a piece of foil pleated across the centre, or a cloth 'cap'. Secure with string.

Place the pudding basin in a steaming basket or colander and steam for about 1½ hours.

SLOW-STEAMED PORK WITH RED CABBAGE

SERVES 4

---

450 g/1 lb RED CABBAGE, THINLY SHREDDED

1 CLOVE OF GARLIC, CRUSHED

1 ONION, THINLY SLICED

10 JUNIPER BERRIES, CRUSHED

SALT AND FRESHLY GROUND BLACK PEPPER

4 THICK, BONELESS LOIN CHOPS

4 TABLESPOONS MARSALA OR PORT

Line the bottom of a steaming basket or colander with foil. Toss together the cabbage, garlic, onion, juniper berries, salt and pepper. Spread half of this mixture over the foil. Place the pork on top, sprinkle with the Marsala or port, then cover with the remaining cabbage mixture. Lay another piece of foil loosely over the top, cover with a lid and steam for about 45 minutes.

Carefully lift the cabbage and pork from the foil. Pour the remaining juices into a saucepan and boil until reduced and the flavour concentrated. To serve, pour the sauce over the cabbage and pork.

GAMMON WITH HONEY AND ORANGE

SERVES 4

Use fresh orange juice from a carton, as it is slightly thicker than home-squeezed orange juice.

———

4 GAMMON STEAKS, ABOUT 150 g/5 oz EACH,
WELL TRIMMED
SLICES OF ORANGE AND SPRIGS OF PARSLEY,
FOR GARNISH

———

MARINADE
150 ml/¼ PINT FRESH ORANGE JUICE
1½ TABLESPOONS CLEAR HONEY
1 TABLESPOON LIME JUICE
2 TEASPOONS SWEET SHERRY
1½ TABLESPOONS WORCESTERSHIRE SAUCE

———

In a medium-sized saucepan, gently warm together the orange juice, honey, lime juice, sherry and Worcestershire sauce. Stir with a wooden spoon until the honey has melted. Allow to cool slightly.

Place the gammon steaks in a shallow, non-metallic dish and pour the marinade over. Cover and leave in a cool place, turning the steaks occasionally, for up to 24 hours.

Take the steaks out of the marinade, allowing the excess liquid to drain off. Place in a steaming basket or colander and steam for 4–5 minutes each side.

In another saucepan, heat the marinade. Pour over the cooked steaks and garnish with slices of orange and sprigs of parsley.

DEVILLED LAMBS' KIDNEYS
SERVES 4

Two 50 g / 2 oz kidneys per portion makes a light dish. For a more substantial meal, either double the number of kidneys and slightly increase the levels of the other ingredients; or use slightly larger kidneys and adjust the cooking time accordingly.

---

8 × 50 g / 2 oz LAMBS' KIDNEYS
1 TABLESPOON TOMATO PURÉE
2 TEASPOONS WORCESTERSHIRE SAUCE
1 TABLESPOON FRENCH MUSTARD
1 TABLESPOON LEMON JUICE

Cut the kidneys in half lengthways and cut out the cores with a pair of scissors.

Mix together the tomato purée, Worcestershire sauce, mustard and lemon juice. Gently coat the pieces of kidney in this mixture. Cover and leave for about 30 minutes.

In a steaming basket or colander, arrange the kidneys in a single layer. Steam for 3 minutes, so they are still pink in the centre; turn the pieces over half-way through so they cook evenly.

Turn off the heat and leave the kidneys in the basket or colander over the steam for a few minutes, to allow the steam to heat through the flesh evenly.

LIVER WITH
MUSHROOMS

SERVES 4

The dried mushrooms add depth and richness to the flavour of this dish, but they are expensive so, unless you're entertaining, use an extra 50–75 g/2–3 oz flat mushrooms.
If sun-dried tomatoes are not available substitute the chopped flesh of 2 well-flavoured tomatoes, boosted with a little tomato purée.

---

1 TEASPOON OLIVE OIL

25 g/1 oz DRIED MUSHROOMS, SOAKED, DRAINED AND CHOPPED

115 g/4 oz FLAT MUSHROOMS, CHOPPED

50 g/2 oz GAMMON, CHOPPED

2 SHALLOTS, FINELY CHOPPED

4 HALVES OF SUN-DRIED TOMATOES PACKED IN OIL, CHOPPED

1 TEASPOON CHOPPED THYME
50 ml/2 fl oz DRY OLOROSO OR MADEIRA

2 TABLESPOONS VEAL STOCK, SEE PAGE 24

SALT AND FRESHLY GROUND BLACK PEPPER

APPROX 575 g/1¼ lb PIECE LAMBS' LIVER

Heat the olive oil in a medium-sized saucepan, add the mushrooms, gammon and shallots and cook for about 4 minutes, stirring occasionally. Stir in the tomato, thyme, oloroso or Madeira, and stock and cook over a low heat for 10 minutes. Season with salt and pepper, leave to cool slightly, then transfer half of the mixture to a large piece of foil. Place the seasoned liver on top and pour the remaining mushroom mixture over. Fold the foil round loosely and tightly seal.

Steam for about 35 minutes then leave the liver to rest for 10 minutes in the foil.

To serve, cut into slices. Spoon over the mushroom mixture and juices from the foil parcel.

SWEETBREADS WITH ASPARAGUS AND TOMATOES

SERVES 4

I think it's a shame that more people are not prepared to eat, let alone cook, sweetbreads as they are delicious and really easy to prepare.
Mangetout can be served in place of asparagus, and wild mushrooms make a good additional ingredient.

---

450 g/1 lb CALVES' SWEETBREADS

1 SMALL CARROT, QUARTERED

1 SHALLOT, HALVED

½ SLIM LEEK, SLICED

1 BAY LEAF

6 BASIL LEAVES

SPRIG OF MARJORAM

3 SPRIGS OF PARSLEY

425 ml/¾ PINT VEAL STOCK, SEE PAGE 24

20 OR 24 SLIM ASPARAGUS TIPS, PEELED

75 g/3 oz PARMA HAM, CULATELLO, WESTPHALIAN OR BAYONNE HAM, WITH FAT REMOVED, CUT INTO STRIPS

1 LARGE, MEDITERRANEAN TOMATO, SKINNED,
SEEDS REMOVED AND DICED
SALT AND FRESHLY GROUND BLACK PEPPER
BASIL LEAVES, FOR GARNISH

————————

Soak the sweetbreads in several changes of cold water for 2–3 hours.
Drain and transfer to a pan of fresh cold water. Bring to the boil and
simmer for 1–2 minutes. Rinse under cold running water. Then, with
a small, sharp knife, carefully remove the covering skin, connective
tissue and gristle, and cut the sweetbreads into slices.

Simmer the carrot, shallot, leek and herbs in the stock for 30
minutes. Steam the asparagus tips over the stock for 8–10 minutes,
until just tender. Remove the asparagus from the basket or colander
and keep warm.

Steam the sweetbreads in the basket or colander over the stock for 3
minutes. Add the ham and tomato to the sweetbreads and steam for a
further 2 minutes. Return the asparagus to the basket or colander,
remove from the pan and keep everything warm.

Simmer the stock until reduced to 115 ml / 4 fl oz. Strain and season
with salt and pepper. Place the sweetbreads, asparagus and ham in the
sauce and serve with the diced tomato and basil leaves scattered over
the top.

VEGETABLES

Steaming is an effortless way of cooking vegetables that are a joy to eat. The cooking starts instantly they are put over the steam, so you avoid the period of semi-cooking which occurs when bringing water-covered vegetables back to the boil. Because they remain stationary, they are not buffeted during cooking (the salvation for potatoes that disintegrate when boiled), and they do not tend to deteriorate so rapidly if left to cook for too long. At the end of steaming, the container holding the vegetables can simply be lifted from the pan, saving the need for straining. It is also much safer than boiling or deep-frying.

It came as no surprise that the vegetables looked attractive and tasted good, but I was delighted by some of the results. The button and cup mushrooms had a flavour and texture that I would not have believed possible, while the fresh flavour and airy, light texture of steamed aubergines lifted them into a class way above their all-too-frequent state of sodden greasiness.

For steaming vegetables you need only a colander, properly covered. If you are cooking a selection for a family or dinner party, you will need two steaming baskets which stack on top of each other.

Always buy the freshest and best quality vegetables possible, no matter how humble or exotic the variety. To ensure even cooking, trim the stalks of sprigs of cauliflower and broccoli, trim asparagus spears and shred cabbage. When cooking Brussels sprouts, select those that are not only the same size but also have similarly-formed heads, bearing in mind that those with tightly packed leaves will take longer to cook than those with loose ones. However, although it is ideal to have uniform vegetables, it is not always feasible so, rather than overcook the smaller ones in order to cook the larger ones sufficiently, start cooking the larger ones first and pop the smaller ones in after some of the cooking time has elapsed.

The cooking times in the recipes and chart will allow the vegetables to remain slightly crisp, but much will depend on the variety, age and structure of a particular vegetable; for example, with celeriac, the coarser layers near the outside take longer than the parts inside.

Vegetable	Size	Steaming time
Asparagus	tips	10–12 mins
	slices 1.25 cm / ½ in	30 secs
Aubergines	halves	8–10 mins
	large cubes	6–7 mins
	slices 0.75 cm / ¼ in	6 mins a side
Beetroot	baby	9–11 mins
Broad beans	young	4–6 mins
	older	8–12 mins
Broccoli	florets	3–4 mins
Brussels sprouts	small	8–10 mins
	medium	10–15 mins
Carrots	new	6–8 mins
older	slices 1.25 cm / ½ in	8–10 mins
Cauliflower	florets	10–15 mins
Celeriac	small cubes	7–8 mins
Courgettes	thin slices	2 mins
Cucumber	rings 2.5 cm / 1 in	4 mins
Fennel	slices 1.25 cm / ½ in	7 mins
French beans		5–8 mins
Girolles		1½ mins
Jerusalem artichokes	small cubes	4–6 mins
Kohlrabi	small cubes	7–9 mins
Mangetout		1½–2 mins
Marrow	large cubes	8–10 mins
Mushrooms	button	3–5 mins
	large cup	6–8 mins
	slices 0.75 cm / ¼ in	2 mins
Onions	approx 15 g / ½ oz each	8–9 mins
Peas		5–8 mins
Potatoes in skins	new/small	18–25 mins

VEGETABLE	SIZE	STEAMING TIME
Old potatoes	175 g / 6 oz	1¾ hours
	thin slices	4 mins
Runner beans	slices 2 cm / ¾ in	5 mins
Salsify	slim	10 mins
Swedes	small cubes	4–6 mins
Turnips	whole baby	7 mins
	strips 1.25 cm / ½ in	2½ mins

ASPARAGUS WITH LEMON BUTTER SAUCE AND OYSTERS

SERVES 4

If oysters are not available, serve strips of smoked salmon, smoked trout fillets, prawns or Parma ham with the asparagus instead.

---

20 ASPARAGUS SPEARS
½ SHALLOT, FINELY CHOPPED
50 ml/2 fl oz DRY WHITE VERMOUTH
50 ml/2 fl oz LEMON JUICE
300 ml/½ PINT CHICKEN STOCK, SEE PAGE 21
50 ml/2 fl oz DOUBLE CREAM
225 g/8 oz UNSALTED BUTTER, DICED
SALT AND FRESHLY GROUND WHITE PEPPER
2 TEASPOONS FINELY GRATED LEMON RIND
8–12 OYSTERS

Trim and discard any woody parts from the stems of the asparagus. Using a vegetable peeler and starting about 4 cm/1½ in from the tips of the asparagus, peel the stems downwards. Chop the peelings finely then boil, with the shallot, in the vermouth and lemon juice until the liquid is reduced to 3 tablespoons. Stir in the stock then steam the asparagus over this liquid for about 10–12 minutes. Remove from the heat and keep warm.

To make the sauce, boil the steaming liquor until reduced to about 115 ml/4 fl oz. Stir in the cream and boil until reduced to about 50 ml/2 fl oz. Strain through a fine sieve and reheat gently.

Over a low heat, gradually whisk in the butter, making sure each piece is fully incorporated before adding the next. Season with salt and pepper, and add the lemon rind. Keep the sauce warm over a very low heat, making sure that it does not boil.

Steam the oysters on the half shell for 30 seconds.
Serve the asparagus and the oysters with the sauce poured over.

ASPARAGUS WITH
SESAME SEEDS

SERVES 4

Asparagus spears vary in thickness so always keep an eye on how the
cooking is progressing.

---

450 g / 1 lb SLIM ASPARAGUS SPEARS
1 TABLESPOON LEMON JUICE
3 TABLESPOONS MILD OLIVE OIL
SALT AND FRESHLY GROUND BLACK PEPPER
1 TABLESPOON SESAME SEEDS, LIGHTLY TOASTED

Trim and discard any woody parts on the stems of the asparagus.
Using a vegetable peeler and starting about 4 cm / 1½ in from the
tips, scrape the stems downwards. Cut the stems diagonally into
1.25 cm / ½ in wide pieces and steam the thicker parts for about
20–30 seconds. Add the thin parts and steam for a further minute or
so, until just crisp.

Whisk together the lemon juice and oil and season with salt and
pepper. Toss the asparagus in the dressing then sprinkle with the
sesame seeds.

AUBERGINES WITH SOY SAUCE AND SESAME SEEDS

SERVES 4

Aubergines steamed are a revelation – they are light with a delicious flavour of their own, and are very low in calories.

---

1 AUBERGINE, ABOUT 225 g/8 oz, CUT INTO APPROX
3 × 2 cm/1¼ × ¾ in PIECES

1 SHALLOT, FINELY CHOPPED

175 ml/6 fl oz FINO SHERRY

2 TABLESPOONS SOY SAUCE

4 TEASPOONS RICE WINE OR SHERRY VINEGAR

2 TABLESPOONS SESAME SEEDS

Steam the aubergine pieces for about 7 minutes, until tender. Remove from the heat and keep warm.

Meanwhile, simmer the shallot in the sherry, soy sauce and rice wine or vinegar until the liquid is reduced to about 4 tablespoons. Stir in the warm pieces of aubergine followed by the sesame seeds.

Transfer to a dish and leave to cool completely.

AUBERGINES WITH SAVOURY TOPPING

SERVES 4

Grappa or brandy helps to 'cut' the richness of the sauce. Neither will make the dish 'alcoholic' as the alcohol disappears with the boiling. But, if you prefer, add lemon juice to taste once the mixture has been boiled instead.

---

2 AUBERGINES, ABOUT 225 g/8 oz EACH

15 g/½ oz UNSALTED BUTTER

1 SMALL SHALLOT, FINELY CHOPPED

75 g/3 oz SLICED RAW SMOKED HAM
EG WESTPHALIAN, FINELY DICED

4 ANCHOVY FILLETS, SOAKED IN MILK FOR
10 MINUTES, DRAINED AND CHOPPED

1½ TABLESPOONS CHOPPED LARGE CAPERS

4 TABLESPOONS GRAPPA OR BRANDY

50 ml/2 fl oz DOUBLE CREAM

FRESHLY GROUND BLACK PEPPER

1 TABLESPOON CHOPPED PARSLEY

Trim the stalks from the aubergines and discard. Cut each aubergine in half lengthways then steam for 8–10 minutes until tender.

Meanwhile, melt the butter in a small saucepan, add the shallot and cook for 2–3 minutes, stirring occasionally. Stir in the ham, heat for a few seconds then add the anchovies and capers. Stir until the anchovies have dissolved. Mix in the grappa or brandy and boil until almost completely evaporated. Add the cream and heat through, still stirring. Season with plenty of freshly ground black pepper.

With the point of a sharp knife, cut 3 or 4 slashes in the surface of each aubergine half. Serve with the sauce poured over and sprinkle with the parsley.

TAHINI-DRESSED BRUSSELS SPROUTS

SERVES 4

Tahini (or sesame seed paste), available from good supermarkets, delicatessens and speciality food stores, adds an interesting, nutty taste to Brussels sprouts.

---

450 g/1 lb SMALL BRUSSELS SPROUTS
300 ml/½ PINT VEGETABLE STOCK, SEE PAGE 26
1 SMALL CLOVE OF GARLIC, CRUSHED
3 TABLESPOONS TAHINI
2 TABLESPOONS LEMON JUICE
APPROX 2 TABLESPOONS LIME JUICE
SALT AND FRESHLY GROUND BLACK PEPPER

Steam the Brussels sprouts over the stock for 7–8 minutes, until just tender. Transfer the sprouts to a serving bowl and keep warm.

To make the dressing, whisk 3 tablespoons of the stock with the garlic, tahini, lemon juice and lime juice. Season with salt and pepper and add more lime juice, if necessary.

To serve, pour the dressing over the sprouts and toss lightly.

CINNAMON CARROTS WITH RAISINS AND PINE NUTS

SERVES 4

The time needed for steaming carrots depends on their age (they should never, of course, be old and woody). The amount of butter can be varied according to how 'buttery' you like vegetables to be. If you are watching the calories the butter can be replaced by a low-fat spread.

---

1 CINNAMON STICK

450 g / 1 lb CARROTS, CUT INTO STRIPS ABOUT
1.25 cm / ½ in WIDE

45 g / 1½ oz RAISINS

45 g / 1½ oz PINE NUTS

APPROX 45 g / 1½ oz UNSALTED BUTTER, DICED
(OPTIONAL)

Add the cinnamon stick to 300 ml / ½ pint water then steam the carrots over this liquid for about 8–10 minutes, until *al dente*.

Toss the carrots with the raisins and pine nuts. Serve with the butter, if used, dotted on top.

CUCUMBER WITH BROAD BEAN PURÉE

SERVES 4

---

225 g/8 oz YOUNG BROAD BEANS
1 LARGE CUCUMBER
50 g/2 oz UNSALTED BUTTER, SOFTENED
2 TABLESPOONS SOURED CREAM
SALT AND FRESHLY GROUND BLACK PEPPER
LEMON JUICE
APPROX 2 TABLESPOONS FINELY CHOPPED
SUMMER SAVORY
SPRIGS OF CHERVIL, FOR GARNISH

Steam the broad beans for 4–6 minutes until tender. Remove from the heat and leave to cool.

Using a canelle knife or a fork, score along the length of the cucumber to give a ridged effect in the skin. Cut the cucumber into 2.5 cm/1 in thick slices and remove the central seeds with an apple corer. Steam the rings for about 4 minutes, until just tender. Remove from the heat and leave to cool.

When the broad beans are cool enough to handle, pop the centres from the outer skins. Purée the centres with the butter and soured cream. Season with salt, pepper and add the lemon juice. Mix in the summer savory and warm the purée through gently.

To serve, place the cucumber rings on a warmed buttered dish and pipe, or spoon, the broad bean purée into the centre of each ring. Garnish with sprigs of chervil.

CAULIFLOWER WITH RED PEPPER SAUCE

SERVES 4

A wonderfully colourful dish that goes particularly well with chicken, turkey or veal.

---

350 ml / 12 fl oz VEGETABLE STOCK, SEE PAGE 26
1 LARGE RED PEPPER, SEEDS REMOVED, DICED
1 SHALLOT, FINELY CHOPPED
1 CLOVE OF GARLIC, CRUSHED (OPTIONAL)
1 CAULIFLOWER, DIVIDED INTO FLORETS
SALT AND FRESHLY GROUND BLACK PEPPER

Add to the stock the red pepper, shallot and garlic, if used. Steam the cauliflower over the stock for about 15–16 minutes, until just tender. Remove from the heat and keep warm.

To make the sauce, boil the stock with the vegetables until reduced to 115 ml / 4 fl oz. Purée, pass through a sieve, adjust the seasoning and reheat if necessary.

To serve, pour most of the sauce around the cauliflower florets with a fine stream over the top.

COURGETTE BOATS

SERVES 4

VEGETABLES FOR STEAMING LIQUID, EG 1 ONION,
1 CARROT, OR 1 STICK OF CELERY, CHOPPED

350 g/12 oz FROZEN PETITS POIS

4 COURGETTES ABOUT 10 cm/4 in LONG

2 SPRIGS OF PARSLEY, COARSELY CHOPPED

3 SPRING ONIONS, CHOPPED

3 TABLESPOONS DOUBLE CREAM

SALT AND FRESHLY GROUND WHITE PEPPER

GRATED NUTMEG

CAYENNE PEPPER

In a steaming basket or colander placed over a steamer or large pan of water containing the onion, carrot or celery, steam the petits pois for 2 minutes and the courgettes for 1½ minutes. Remove the courgettes from the basket or colander and slice lengthways. Carefully scoop out the seeds using a teaspoon. Purée the peas, half of the parsley, the spring onions and cream, to make a slightly grainy consistency. Season with salt, pepper, nutmeg and cayenne pepper and divide the mixture between the courgette shells. Sprinkle the remaining parsley on top and steam again for 10 minutes.

FRENCH BEAN BUNDLES
SERVES 4

Strips of red pepper make these French bean bundles look extra
attractive.

---

350 g / 12 oz SLIM FRENCH BEANS (HARICOTS VERTS)
4 LONG STRIPS OF CHIVES OR GREEN PART OF LEEK
OR SPRING ONION
4 LONG STRIPS OF RED PEPPER (OPTIONAL)
4–6 SPRIGS OF SUMMER SAVORY

Group the beans into bundles. Place the strips of chives, leek or spring
onion and red pepper, if used, in a colander and pour boiling water
through. Drain well and use to tie up the bundles of beans, finishing
with a knot, or a bow if your fingers are nimble enough. Add the sprigs
of summer savory to a steamer or large pan of boiling water then steam
the bean bundles over this liquid for about 7–9 minutes, until still
crisp.

KOHLRABI WITH
TOMATOES AND LIGHT
HERB MOUSSELINE
SAUCE
SERVES 4–6

It should not be necessary to peel small kohlrabi before they are
cooked, but the tough skins of larger ones must be removed. If only
large ones are available, buy up to 225 g / 8 oz more to compensate
for the amount that will be lost in peeling. The sauce is made in the
same way as mayonnaise, and the best results are achieved by using a
blender.

---

2 BAY LEAVES, BROKEN IN HALF

1 BUNCH OF PARSLEY

2 SPRIGS OF LOVAGE OR LEAVES FROM 2 STICKS OF CELERY

700 g/1½ lb SMALL KOHLRABI, STALKS AND LEAVES REMOVED, CUT INTO APPROX 0.75 mm/¼ in SLICES

350 g/12 oz TOMATOES, SKINNED AND SEEDS REMOVED, CHOPPED

1 EGG YOLK

2 TEASPOONS DIJON MUSTARD

1 TABLESPOON GRATED LIME RIND

APPROX 3 TABLESPOONS LIME JUICE

115 ml/4 fl oz GOOD OLIVE OIL, PREFERABLY EXTRA VIRGIN

5 TABLESPOONS WHIPPING CREAM, LIGHTLY WHIPPED

SALT AND FRESHLY GROUND BLACK PEPPER

FINELY CHOPPED LOVAGE OR PARSLEY, FOR GARNISH

Put the herbs into a steamer or large pan and pour in 200 ml/7 fl oz boiling water. Steam the kohlrabi over this liquid for about 7–8 minutes, adding the tomato a minute before the end of the cooking. Remove from the heat and keep warm. Strain the liquid and reserve.

For the sauce, mix together the egg yolk, mustard, lime rind and 1 teaspoon of the lime juice. Very gradually whisk in the oil, as for making mayonnaise, then gradually whisk in 5 tablespoons of the stock. Fold in the cream, season and add more lime juice to taste.

Transfer the vegetables to a warmed dish and pour the sauce over. Sprinkle with finely chopped lovage or parsley and serve immediately.

SPLIT LEEKS FILLED WITH WHEAT AND CHEESE

SERVES 4

If you prefer, other well-flavoured cheeses can be used instead of goats' cheese. Soft types are best, but if you use a hard cheese, grate it finely unless it is a blue variety, which is better crumbled.

---

50 g/2 oz WHOLE WHEAT, SOAKED OVERNIGHT

SPRIG OF THYME

4 LONG LEEKS, WHITE PART ABOUT 12.5 cm/5 in
LONG × 2.5 cm/1 in DIAMETER, OUTER LEAVES
REMOVED, TRIMMED

50 g/2 oz GOATS' CHEESE WITHOUT RIND, CHOPPED

1½ TABLESPOONS SINGLE CREAM

2 TEASPOONS LEMON JUICE

1 TABLESPOON CHOPPED LARGE CAPERS

SALT AND FRESHLY GROUND BLACK PEPPER

SPRIGS OF THYME, FOR GARNISH

First, drain the wheat. Add a sprig of thyme to a large saucepan of water and cook the wheat gently for 35 minutes, until just tender.

Meanwhile, with the point of a sharp knife, make a cut along the length of each leek, almost right the way through. Open out the leeks then steam over the pan of wheat for about 5 minutes, until cooked but still crisp. Remove the leeks from the heat and keep warm.

Drain the wheat. Mix in the cheese, cream, lemon juice, capers, salt and plenty of black pepper. Divide the mixture between the leeks and garnish with several small sprigs of thyme.

MANGETOUT WITH COCONUT

SERVES 4

This recipe can be varied in a number of ways: use sesame oil or 25 g / 1 oz melted unsalted butter instead of walnut oil, coriander instead of parsley, and French beans instead of mangetout.

---

1 SMALL ONION, FINELY CHOPPED

450 g / 1 lb MANGETOUT, TRIMMED

2 TABLESPOONS WALNUT OR HAZELNUT OIL, HEATED

40 g / 1½ oz GRATED FRESH OR DESICCATED COCONUT, LIGHTLY TOASTED

2 TABLESPOONS CHOPPED PARSLEY

Steam the onion over seasoned water for 4–5 minutes until soft. Remove from the heat and keep warm. Steam the mangetout for 1½–2 minutes. If there is room in the steaming basket or colander or on the rack the mangetout and onion can be steamed at the same time but keep them separate.

Mix the onion lightly with the oil, coconut and parsley.

Transfer the mangetout to a warmed serving dish and sprinkle with the coconut mixture.

STUFFED MUSHROOMS

SERVES 4

Serve as a light first course with a small garnish of crisp salad leaves and crusty or wholemeal bread. If the mushrooms have long stems use the part that is nearest the cap.

---

8 MUSHROOMS, ABOUT 5 cm/2 in DIAMETER
2 COURGETTES, ABOUT 75 g/3 oz EACH, FINELY GRATED
SCANT 1 TEASPOON HORSERADISH RELISH
1 EGG YOLK, BEATEN
1 TEASPOON SOURED CREAM OR TOP-OF-THE MILK
SALT AND FRESHLY GROUND BLACK PEPPER
CHICKEN STOCK FOR STEAMING (OPTIONAL), SEE PAGE 21

Wipe the outsides of the mushrooms with a damp cloth, if necessary. Remove the stems from the mushrooms, trim and chop finely. Mix in a bowl with the courgettes, horseradish, egg yolk, and soured cream or top-of-the milk.

Season the insides and outsides of the mushroom caps. Divide the courgette mixture between the caps and steam over the chicken stock, or seasoned water, for about 7 minutes, so that the mushrooms still retain a little 'bite'. Serve immediately.

MUSHROOMS WITH HERB SAUCE

SERVES 4–6

Steaming is by far the best way of cooking mushrooms as it not only retains their shape and texture but also enhances their flavour.

---

350 g/12 oz BUTTON MUSHROOMS, STALKS REMOVED
UNLESS VERY SMALL

2–3 SMALL, YOUNG SPRIGS OF ROSEMARY

SALT AND FRESHLY GROUND BLACK PEPPER

1 SHALLOT, FINELY CHOPPED

300 ml/½ PINT CHICKEN OR VEGETABLE STOCK, SEE
PAGES 21 OR 26

1 TABLESPOON FINELY CHOPPED TARRAGON

1 TABLESPOON FINELY CHOPPED PARSLEY

150 ml/¼ PINT DOUBLE CREAM

2 TEASPOONS HERB MUSTARD

15 g/½ oz UNSALTED BUTTER, DICED

LEMON JUICE

SMALL SPRIGS OF TARRAGON, FOR GARNISH

Lay the mushroom caps, dome-side uppermost, in a single layer in a steaming basket or colander.

Add the rosemary, salt and pepper and shallot to the stock and steam the mushrooms over this liquid for about 3–5 minutes, so they lose their 'rawness' but retain some 'bite'. Remove the basket or colander from the pan and keep the mushrooms warm.

To make the sauce, boil the stock until reduced to 75 ml/3 fl oz. Remove the rosemary and add the chopped herbs and cream. Boil until thick enough to coat the back of a spoon, then add the mustard. Swirl in the butter, making sure each piece is incorporated before adding the next, season to taste and add sufficient lemon juice to make the sauce sharp without being acid.

Stir in the mushrooms and serve garnished with small sprigs of tarragon.

JERUSALEM ARTICHOKES WITH PARMA HAM

SERVES 4

This sauce is difficult to make in smaller quantities, so if you find that you have too much for this dish, keep the remainder covered, in a cool place.

---

900 g / 2 lb SMOOTH JERUSALEM ARTICHOKES, PEELED, CUT INTO 1.5 cm / ½ in SLICES

300 ml / ½ PINT VEAL STOCK FOR STEAMING (OPTIONAL), SEE PAGE 24

75 g / 3 oz PARMA HAM OR WELL-FLAVOURED SMOKED GAMMON, DICED

1 TABLESPOON WHOLE-GRAIN MUSTARD

2 EGG YOLKS

50 ml / 2 fl oz SOURED CREAM

SALT AND FRESHLY GROUND BLACK PEPPER

APPROX 1 TABLESPOON LEMON JUICE

Steam the artichokes over the boiling veal stock, or seasoned water, for 4–5 minutes, until crisp. Remove the artichokes from the heat and keep warm. Steam the ham or gammon for about 2 minutes, remove the steaming container from the pan and keep the ham or gammon warm.

If veal stock has been used for the steaming, boil 115 ml / 4 fl oz until it is reduced to 2 tablespoons. Stir the mustard into the reduced stock, or 2 tablespoons of the boiling steaming water, then stir into a bowl containing the egg yolks. Whisk over a saucepan of hot water until thickened. Add the soured cream and season with salt and pepper. Add a little lemon juice to 'lift' the flavour, if necessary.

To serve, toss the Jerusalem artichokes with the ham or gammon and pour the sauce over.

BUTTERED STEAMED PARSLEY

SERVES 4

Buttered steamed parsley makes a good side dish.

———————

75 g/3 oz PARSLEY, STALKS REMOVED
50 g/2 oz UNSALTED BUTTER, DICED
2 TEASPOONS LEMON JUICE
SALT AND FRESHLY GROUND BLACK PEPPER

———————

Steam the parsley for 1 minute.

Meanwhile, melt the butter. Stir in the lemon juice, and season with salt and pepper. Transfer the cooked parsley to a warmed dish and fluff it up lightly. Sprinkle the butter mixture over and fork through. Serve immediately.

PEAS STEAMED WITH LETTUCE

SERVES 4

This recipe is based on the traditional way of cooking peas with lettuce, known as *à la française*. The addition of spring onions and red pepper gives a dash of colour as well as flavour.

APPROX 450 g/1 lb FRESH PEAS IN THE POD, TO YIELD
ABOUT 225 g/8 oz WHEN SHUCKED

3 SPRING ONIONS, SLICED

SMALL HEAD OF LETTUCE, SHREDDED

4 SPRIGS OF MINT

SALT AND FRESHLY GROUND BLACK PEPPER

3 TABLESPOONS CHOPPED RED PEPPER

KNOB OF UNSALTED BUTTER, FOR SERVING
(OPTIONAL)

Shuck the peas. Mix with the spring onions and lettuce, then place in a steaming basket or colander. Place the sprigs of mint and the seasoning in a steamer or large saucepan of water. Steam the pea mixture over this for about 4 minutes. Stir in the red pepper and steam for another 3 minutes or so until the peas are just tender.

Transfer to a warmed serving dish and top with a knob of unsalted butter, if liked.

STUFFED PEPPERS
SERVES 4

Insert wooden cocktail sticks in the shape of a cross through the
bottom of each pepper to make it stand upright during steaming.
The vast majority of couscous now on sale is pre-cooked.

———————

4 GREEN OR RED PEPPERS, ABOUT 100 g/3½ oz EACH
1 SHALLOT, FINELY CHOPPED
1 CLOVE OF GARLIC, CRUSHED
4 TABLESPOONS FINELY CHOPPED PARSLEY
PINCH OF CHOPPED OREGANO
4 BEEFSTEAK OR OTHER LARGE, FULL-FLAVOURED
TOMATOES, SKINNED AND SEEDS
REMOVED, CHOPPED
1½ TEASPOONS TOMATO PURÉE
4 TABLESPOONS CHOPPED, STONED BLACK OLIVES
2 TABLESPOONS CHOPPED CAPERS
2 TABLESPOONS PRE-COOKED COUSCOUS, SOAKED
FOR 20 MINUTES IN COLD WATER
8 ANCHOVY FILLETS, SOAKED IN COLD MILK
THEN DRAINED
SALT AND FRESHLY GROUND BLACK PEPPER

———————

Using a small sharp knife, cut around the stems of the peppers and
remove, leaving as small an opening as possible. Pull out and discard
the cores and use a teaspoon to remove the seeds and white flesh.

Steam the shallot and garlic for about 4–5 minutes until soft, then
mix in a bowl with the parsley, oregano, tomato flesh, tomato purée,
olives and capers.

Drain the couscous and squeeze out as much water as possible. Stir
into the tomato mixture and add the anchovies. Season with plenty of
black pepper but only a little salt.

Divide this mixture into 4 and use to stuff each of the peppers. Steam for 25–35 minutes, depending how soft you like the pepper flesh to be.

ANCHOVY POTATO SLICES

SERVES 4–6

These savoury slices make a tasty accompaniment to steamed meats and fish and also go well served with Red Pepper Sauce (see page 183). Alternative flavourings include herb, garlic or pepper flavoured soft cheese, finely grated cheese, mustard, yeast extract, horseradish sauce or relish.

---

4 SMALL – MEDIUM-SIZED POTATOES, CUT INTO APPROX 4 mm/⅙ in THICK SLICES

GENTLEMAN'S RELISH

Spread half of the potato slices fairly thinly with Gentleman's Relish then place the other slices on top. Steam for about 8 minutes, or until just tender.

JACKET POTATOES WITH LEEKS

SERVES 4

---

4 POTATOES, ABOUT 175 g/6 oz EACH, WITH THEIR
SKINS INTACT AND CLEANED

225 g/8 oz WHITE PART OF LEEK, SLICED

2 TABLESPOONS GREEK YOGHURT OR OTHER
THICK YOGHURT

APPROX 2 TEASPOONS CREAMED HORSERADISH

50 g/2 oz MATURE CHEDDAR CHEESE, GRATED

SALT AND FRESHLY GROUND BLACK PEPPER

Steam the potatoes for about 1¾ hours, turning them over two or three times, or until tender. Remove from the heat and keep warm.

Steam the leeks for about 4–5 minutes until tender. Remove from the steaming container and keep warm.

Cut the potatoes into halves, lengthways, and carefully scoop out the flesh, leaving a thin shell of skin. Purée the flesh with the leeks, yoghurt, horseradish cream and cheese. Season with salt and pepper to taste, and adjust the level of horseradish if necessary.

Divide the potato mixture between the potato shells and steam again for about 10 minutes, until heated through.

SALSIFY WITH LEMON SAUCE

SERVES 4

The sauce, which is light with a distinctive clean lemon flavour,
makes a very good contrast to the salsify. Be careful not to overdo
the sugar – about 2–3 teaspoons should be enough.

---

450 g/1 lb SALSIFY

JUICE AND THE RIND, IN LONG PIECES, FROM 1
LEMON

75 ml/3 fl oz DRY WHITE VERMOUTH

3 WHITE PEPPERCORNS, LIGHTLY CRUSHED

350 ml/12 fl oz VEGETABLE OR CHICKEN STOCK, SEE
PAGES 26 OR 21

150 g/5 oz FROMAGE BLANC

1 EGG YOLK

SALT AND FRESHLY GROUND WHITE PEPPER

SUGAR, TO TASTE

SMALL SPRIGS OF THYME OR PARSLEY, FOR GARNISH

Peel the salsify, cut each one into narrow lengths and toss in lemon
juice immediately. Add the lemon rind, vermouth and peppercorns to
the stock and steam the salsify over this liquor for about 10 minutes, or
until just tender – the time will depend on the thickness of the pieces.
Remove the steaming container from the pan, keep the salsify covered
and warm.

To make the sauce, boil the steaming liquor until reduced to
50 ml/2 fl oz. Remove the lemon rind and peppercorns. In a bowl,
mix the fromage blanc with the egg yolk, then stir in a little of the
liquor. Pour into a food processor or blender with the remaining
liquid and mix together well. Return to the pan.

Heat gently, stirring with a wooden spoon, until lightly thickened –

do not allow to boil. Season with salt and white pepper and add sugar to taste.

To serve, spoon a trickle of sauce over the salsify and the rest beside it. Garnish with small sprigs of thyme or parsley.

TURNIPS WITH APPLE AND ORANGE BUTTER SAUCE

SERVES 3–4

Serve on a bed of crisp curly endive or iceberg lettuce as a first course, or as a luxurious vegetable accompaniment to plainly cooked meats.

---

300 g/10 oz PREPARED YOUNG TURNIPS, CUT INTO STRIPS ABOUT 1.25 cm/½ in WIDE

1 CRISP, GREEN APPLE, CORED AND CUT INTO STRIPS ABOUT 7.5 mm/¼ in WIDE

2 TEASPOONS SUNFLOWER SEEDS

SAUCE

1 SHALLOT, FINELY CHOPPED

50 ml/2 fl oz WHITE WINE VINEGAR

50 ml/2 fl oz ORANGE JUICE

115 ml/4 fl oz FULL-BODIED DRY WHITE WINE

115 g/4 oz UNSALTED BUTTER, DICED

2 TEASPOONS FRESHLY GRATED ORANGE RIND

SALT AND FRESHLY GROUND BLACK PEPPER

In a small saucepan boil the shallot for the sauce in the vinegar, orange juice and wine until reduced to 25 ml/1 fl oz.

Steam the turnip strips over seasoned water for about 2½ minutes, so they remain crisp.

Lower the heat beneath the sauce and gradually whisk in the butter, making sure each piece is fully incorporated before adding the next. Add the orange rind and season with salt and pepper to taste.

Toss the cooked turnips with the apple, pour the sauce over and toss with the sunflower seeds. Serve immediately.

SWEET SPICED TURNIPS
SERVES 4

The combination of butter, honey and cumin makes the turnips sweet and spicy. The amounts of butter, honey and cumin can be varied to taste.

———————

4 SMALL PEELED TURNIPS, ABOUT 50–75 g/2–3 oz EACH
APPROX 25 g/1 oz BUTTER, SOFTENED
2–3 TEASPOONS SET HONEY, TO TASTE
APPROX ½ TEASPOON GROUND CUMIN, TO TASTE
SALT AND FRESHLY GROUND BLACK PEPPER

———————

Place each turnip on a piece of foil. Mix together the butter, honey, cumin, salt and pepper, then divide into 4 and put over the turnips. Fold the foil up round the turnips to make tightly sealed but loose parcels and steam for about 10 minutes, until the turnips are just becoming tender but still retain some 'bite'.

SPICED RED CABBAGE
SERVES 4

___

450 g/1 lb RED CABBAGE, COARSE STEMS REMOVED,
THINLY SLICED
1 DESSERT APPLE, PEELED, CORED AND SLICED
1 ONION, SLICED
5 CLOVES
SALT AND FRESHLY GROUND BLACK PEPPER
2 TEASPOONS SHERRY VINEGAR
1 TEASPOON REDCURRANT JELLY

___

Toss together the cabbage, apple, onion, cloves and salt and pepper.

Line a steaming basket or colander with greaseproof paper and place the cabbage mixture on top.

Blend the vinegar into the jelly then sprinkle over the cabbage. Cover with a sheet of greaseproof paper and steam for about 45 minutes, until the cabbage is very tender.

If there is a lot of excess liquid with the cabbage, carefully pour or spoon it into a small saucepan. Boil it down until reduced and concentrated, then stir it back into the cabbage.

VEGETABLE CABBAGE STRUDEL

SERVES 4

---

1 MEDIUM-SIZED SAVOY CABBAGE

115 g/4 oz CARROTS, STEAMED

½ CELERIAC, CUT INTO STRIPS 2 cm/¾ in WIDE, STEAMED FOR 5 MINUTES

115 g/4 oz BUTTON MUSHROOMS, SLICED AND STEAMED FOR 2 MINUTES

115 g/4 oz BROCCOLI FLORETS, STEAMED FOR 7 MINUTES

150 g/5 oz COARSELY GRATED GRUYÈRE CHEESE

PINCH OF CARAWAY SEEDS (OPTIONAL)

SALT AND FRESHLY GROUND BLACK PEPPER

RED PEPPER SAUCE, SEE PAGE 183, OR HERB OR MUSTARD HOLLANDAISE, SEE PAGE 28, TO SERVE

Remove the outer leaves from the cabbage and blanch for 45–60 seconds so they become soft enough to roll. Cut the inner yellow part into chunks and steam for about 2–3 minutes, or until just softened.

Lay the cabbage leaves out on a large piece of cheesecloth, over-lapping them slightly so there are no gaps. Cover with layers of

vegetables, including the cabbage heart, and cheese and add a sprinkling of caraway seeds, if used. Season with salt and pepper.

With the help of the cloth, roll the mixture up from a short side, like a Swiss roll, enclosing it in the cloth. Twist the ends of the cloth to secure. Carefully transfer to a steaming basket rack or colander, curving the roll slightly if necessary, and steam for about 35–40 minutes.

Lift the cloth-covered roll from the steaming container and remove the cloth – take care as it will be hot.

Serve sliced, with Red Pepper Sauce or Herb or Mustard Hollandaise.

PUDDINGS AND DESSERTS

Mention steaming in this country and most people's minds will instantly conjure up a large suet pudding. But, apart from the fact that a good steamed sponge is as light as air, there are infinitely more puddings that can be made by steaming.

The Chinese even steam cakes very similar to our whisked or cream sponge mixtures. Inspired by this, but also slightly sceptical, I thought I would try steaming a new, very delicate, light walnut cake, quite prepared for a failure. But no – a triumph. The steam is even, so there is no need to worry about whether the oven temperature is too high or too low or whether certain parts of the oven are hotter than others. The main point to remember when steaming this type of pudding or cake is that if it takes more than 7–10 minutes to cook, grease-proof paper should be laid over the top to protect it from drips of condensation.

Traditional recipes can be given a new look and new appeal by cooking them in mouthful-sized portions in small containers such as sake cups. These puddings are elegant enough for a dinner party and especially popular with people who like steamed puddings but find that by the end of a meal they haven't got room for them. You can either serve two or three small puddings of all one flavour or you can divide the basic mixture into two or three, add a different flavouring to each portion and cook them separately so each guest can be served with a selection.

Egg custard mixtures, either plain or flavoured, can be steamed if cooked in individual containers or shallow layers using, for example, a flan tin. Line the steaming basket with foil or greaseproof paper to prevent the bottom from cooking too quickly, whilst a sheet of greaseproof paper over the top stops condensation dripping from the lid on to the mixture.

It is far easier and healthier to steam fruit rather than to cook it by poaching or stewing. Not only does the fruit stay stationary, so remaining whole – rhubarb that is cooked to tenderness yet stays in whole pieces is indeed a rare treat – but also the fruit retains its soluble nutrients and flavour.

Flavour the steaming water with spices, vanilla pods, lemon balm, elderflowers and so on, and the fragrant steam will permeate the fruit both during the cooking and if left to cool over the liquor afterwards.

CINNAMON-SCENTED PEARS WITH RUM AND ORANGE SAUCE

SERVES 4

---

1 CINNAMON STICK

4 FIRM DESSERT PEARS

2 EGG YOLKS

150 ml/¼ PINT MILK

150 g/5 oz FROMAGE BLANC OR 150 ml/¼ PINT THICK PLAIN YOGHURT

2 TABLESPOONS RUM

2 TEASPOONS FINELY GRATED ORANGE RIND

APPROX 25 g/1 oz VANILLA SUGAR, TO TASTE

Pour 300 ml/½ pint water into the bottom of a steamer or large saucepan, add the cinnamon stick and bring slowly to the boil.

Peel and core the pears and cut into approximately 1.25 cm/½ in slices. Place the slices in a single layer over the base of a steaming basket or large colander and steam over the cinnamon liquid for 7–8

minutes, until just tender. Remove the basket or colander from the pan and keep the pears warm.

Meanwhile, make the sauce. Mix together in a bowl the egg yolks with the milk and fromage blanc or yoghurt. Place the bowl over a saucepan of hot, but not boiling, water and whisk the mixture until it thickens. Remove from the heat and whisk in the rum, orange rind and vanilla sugar to taste.

Serve the warm slices of pear with the warm sauce.

PEAR AND GUAVA CHARLOTTE

SERVES 4

---

900 g/2 lb PEARS, PEELED, CORED AND ROUGHLY
CHOPPED

1 RIPE GUAVA, PEELED AND CHOPPED

JUICE AND GRATED RIND OF 1 LEMON

50 g/2 oz UNSALTED BUTTER

50 g/2 oz GRANULATED SUGAR

APPROX 5 SLICES FROM A LARGE WHITE LOAF,
CRUSTS REMOVED

50 g/2 oz UNSALTED BUTTER, MELTED

SOFT LIGHT BROWN SUGAR

CRÈME FRAÎCHE, FROMAGE BLANC OR THICK PLAIN
YOGHURT, TO SERVE

Place the pears and guava in a saucepan. Pour in the lemon juice, cover and cook gently until the fruit juices begin to run. Add the butter, lemon rind and granulated sugar, and cook until the fruit is soft and the surplus liquid has evaporated. Stir the mixture with a wooden spoon towards the end of the cooking to prevent it sticking. Increase the heat if necessary to drive off excess liquid.

Cut one slice of bread to fit into the bottom of a 900 ml/1½ pint charlotte mould or 12.5 cm/5 in cake tin, and another one to fit the top. Brush the charlotte mould or tin with melted butter, and coat the sides and bottom liberally with soft brown sugar. Dip each piece of bread into the remaining butter and use to line neatly the mould or tin, making sure there are no gaps.

Spoon the fruit into the mould. Cover with the remaining piece of shaped bread. Lay a sheet of greaseproof paper on top and steam for an hour.

Remove from the heat but leave the pudding to stand for several minutes before turning out.

Serve warm with crème fraîche, fromage blanc or thick plain yoghurt.

CLOVE-FLAVOURED APPLE SLICES WITH VANILLA SAUCE

SERVES 4

450 g/1 lb BRAMLEY'S SEEDLING APPLES
7–8 CLOVES
SUGAR, TO TASTE

VANILLA SAUCE
1 VANILLA POD, SPLIT
250 ml/9 fl oz MILK, OR HALF MILK/HALF
SINGLE CREAM
2 EGG YOLKS
APPROX 20 g/¾ oz CASTER SUGAR

Add the vanilla pod to the milk then bring slowly to just below simmering point. Cover, remove from the heat and leave to infuse for 20 minutes.

During that time, peel and core the apples, then cut into 1.5 cm/ ½ in slices. Pour 300 ml/ ½ pint water into the bottom of a steamer or large saucepan, add the cloves and bring to the boil. Steam over this liquid for about 5 minutes, until just tender.

Meanwhile, remove the vanilla pod from the milk and heat the milk to just below simmering point. In a bowl, mix the egg yolks with the sugar using a wooden spoon, then gradually stir in the milk. Pour the sauce back into the rinsed pan and heat very gently, stirring constantly, until thickened.

Sprinkle a little sugar to taste over the apple slices and serve warm with the custard.

STUFFED APPLES

SERVES 4

Amaretto, an almond-flavoured liqueur, can be bought in miniature bottles but, if you prefer, sherry, whisky, rum, brandy or an orange liqueur can be used instead. Or perhaps a blend of spirit and liqueur.

––––––––––

16 DRIED APRICOTS, CHOPPED
5 TABLESPOONS AMARETTO
4 COOKING APPLES, ABOUT 225 g/8 oz EACH

––––––––––

Place the apricots in a small saucepan, add the liqueur, cover and heat gently for 5 minutes. Remove from the heat and leave to soak for several hours.

Core the apples then, with the point of a sharp knife, score just through the skin, around the circumference of each apple. Place each one in the centre of a piece of foil large enough to enclose it completely. Divide the apricots and any remaining liquor between the cavities in the apples, then fold the foil loosely around them, sealing the joins well.

Steam for 20–25 minutes, depending on the size of the apples and how soft you like them to be.

ANGELICA RHUBARB
SERVES 4–6

Vanilla sugar gives a soft, subtle sweetness and is simplicity itself to make. Simply put a vanilla pod in with the sugar during storage.

———————

HANDFUL OF FRESH ANGELICA LEAVES WITH
SHORT STALKS

450 g/1 lb SLIM RHUBARB, CUT INTO APPROX
3.75 cm/1½ in LENGTHS

SUGAR

225 g/8 oz FROMAGE FRAIS, CHILLED

150 ml/¼ PINT CHILLED CRÈME FRAÎCHE, WHIPPED
UNTIL THICK BUT NOT STIFF

APPROX 15 g/½ oz VANILLA SUGAR, TO TASTE

1 EGG WHITE, WHISKED UNTIL STIFF BUT NOT DRY

CRYSTALLIZED ANGELICA

———————

Bruise the stalks of the angelica leaves lightly, then spread out in a layer on the bottom of a steaming basket or on a fine-meshed rack. Place a layer of rhubarb on top and cover with more angelica leaves. Steam for about 3–4 minutes, until the rhubarb is almost tender. Turn off the heat and leave until cool. Sweeten lightly.

Gently fold the fromage frais into the crème fraîche and add a little vanilla sugar to taste. Fold in the egg white, then taste again as the egg white will dull the sweetness – however, the mixture should not be too sweet.

Make a bed out of the cold fromage frais mixture. Place the cooled but not cold rhubarb on top and sprinkle with crystallized angelica.

STUFFED FIGS
SERVES 4

---

8 LARGE FIRM BLACK FIGS
100 g/3½ oz SOFT CHEESE
1 TABLESPOON GROUND ALMONDS
2 TABLESPOONS FINELY GRATED ORANGE RIND
3 TABLESPOONS SOFT LIGHT BROWN SUGAR
THICK GREEK YOGHURT, TO SERVE

Cut the top quarter or third from each fig, then make a deep indentation in the bottom section.

Beat the cheese to soften, then mix in the ground almonds, orange rind and sugar. Divide this mixture into 8 and use to fill the indentations in the figs, pressing the filling in lightly. Cover with the tops and steam the figs for about 5–7 minutes, until just tender.

Remove the figs from the heat and leave to cool. Serve while just warm, or cold, with thick Greek yoghurt.

GOOSEBERRIES WITH ELDERFLOWERS

SERVES 4

The light texture and flavour of lightly chilled fromage frais goes very well with these gooseberries, which are delicately flavoured with elderflowers.

SEVERAL SPRIGS OF ELDERFLOWERS
450 g/1 lb DESSERT GOOSEBERRIES
CASTER SUGAR (OPTIONAL)
LIGHTLY CHILLED FROMAGE FRAIS, TO SERVE
SMALL SPRIGS OF ELDERFLOWERS, FOR DECORATION

Spread out a layer of elderflower sprigs on the bottom of a steaming basket or on a fine-meshed rack. Place the gooseberries on top in a single layer and cover with more elderflowers. Steam for about 3–4 minutes, depending on size, ripeness and variety of the gooseberries, until lightly cooked.

Remove from the heat and leave to cool.

Sprinkle the gooseberries with a little caster sugar, if necessary, and serve with a bowl of lightly chilled fromage frais, decorated with elderflowers.

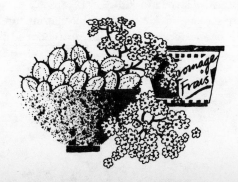

VANILLA PEACHES
SERVES 4

After use, rinse and dry the vanilla pod so that it can be used again.

---

4 FIRM PEACHES, HALVED AND STONED
1 VANILLA POD
150 g/5 oz COTTAGE CHEESE, SIEVED
50 g/2 oz HIGH- OR LOW-FAT SOFT CHEESE, SIEVED
1 OR 2 DROPS OF ORANGE FLOWER WATER
40 g/1½ oz PISTACHIO NUTS, FINELY CHOPPED
ICING SUGAR OR SWEETENER, TO TASTE
CHOPPED PISTACHIO NUTS, FOR DECORATION

Place the peach halves, dome-side uppermost, in a single layer in a steaming basket or colander.

Pour 300 ml/½ pint water into the bottom of a steamer or large pan, add the vanilla pod and bring to the boil. Steam the peaches over the water for about 4 minutes. Remove from the heat, then carefully skin the peaches. Steam the halves, dome-side down, for about another 4 minutes. Turn off the heat and leave the peaches to cool. Cover and chill.

Beat together the cottage cheese, soft cheese and orange flower water, until smooth. Add the nuts and sufficient icing sugar or sweetener to taste. Cover and chill.

Just before serving, divide the pistachio nut mixture between the cavities in the peaches and sprinkle with extra chopped pistachio nuts.

LIGHT LIME SOUFFLÉS

SERVES 4

Serve these light, refreshing soufflés after a rich meal or whenever you want a simple dessert.

---

350 g/12 oz RICOTTA CHEESE, SIEVED
40g/1½ oz SUGAR
FINELY GRATED RIND OF 4 LIMES
JUICE OF 2 LIMES
3 EGG WHITES, WHISKED

Beat the cheese with the sugar, then add the lime rind and juice. Lightly fold in the egg whites, then divide the mixture between 4 heatproof ramekin dishes. Steam for about 8–10 minutes. Serve immediately.

CUSTARD RINGS

SERVES 4

The smooth, 'creamy' texture of this dessert makes it taste deceptively rich. It can either be served warm or cold, on its own or with summer fruits, such as strawberries, raspberries, loganberries or blackcurrants; with steamed slices of well-flavoured eating apple, such as Cox's Orange Pippin or Washington Red; with steamed slices of pear. If using the last two fruits a pinch of grated nutmeg or ground cinnamon added to the custard is particularly good.

300 g/10 oz FROMAGE BLANC
4 EGG YOLKS
2 TABLESPOONS CASTER SUGAR
PINCH OF FRESHLY GRATED NUTMEG (OPTIONAL)

Stir the fromage blanc into the egg yolks until smooth, then add the sugar and a pinch of nutmeg, if used.

Divide the mixture between 4 lightly buttered ring moulds then steam for about 6–7 minutes, until just set.

Leave the custards in the rings for a few minutes before carefully turning out. Serve warm or cold.

ALMOND AND CARDAMOM SPONGE WITH APRICOT CREAM

SERVES 6

The cold tang of the sauce contrasts with the warm spice of the pudding, making a deliciously 'moreish' combination.

100 g/3½ oz GROUND ALMONDS
175 g/6 oz UNSALTED BUTTER, SOFTENED
75 g/3 oz CASTER SUGAR
75 g/3 oz SOFT LIGHT BROWN SUGAR
SEEDS FROM 4 LARGE GREEN CARDAMOM PODS, CRUSHED
3 EGGS, BEATEN
100 g/3½ oz SELF-RAISING FLOUR

APRICOT CREAM

225 g/8 oz DRIED APRICOTS, SOAKED OVERNIGHT
JUICE AND FINELY GRATED RIND OF 1 SMALL
ORANGE
150 ml/¼ PINT SOURED CREAM
50 g/2 oz FLAKED ALMONDS, TOASTED

Sprinkle 1 tablespoon ground almonds into a lightly oiled 1.5 litre/ 2½ pint pudding basin, shaking the basin to coat the side and base evenly.

Cream together the butter, sugars and cardamon seeds, until very light and fluffy. Gradually add the eggs, beating well after each addition and shaking in a little of the flour towards the end. Fold in the remaining flour and ground almonds. Spoon into the basin. Cover the top of the pudding with a piece of buttered greaseproof paper, then cover the basin with a piece of foil pleated across the centre and secure with string. Steam for about 2 hours or until a skewer inserted into the centre comes out clean.

To make the apricot cream, drain the apricots and reserve the soaking liquor. Purée the fruit with the orange rind and juice (made up to 150 ml/¼ pint with the soaking liquor) to give a thick pouring consistency; add more of the liquor if necessary. Whisk in the soured cream then cover and chill.

Turn the pudding out on to a warm plate, spoon some of the apricot cream on top so that it runs down the sides and sprinkle with the toasted flaked almonds. Serve the remaining apricot cream separately.

WARM HAZELNUT MOUSSES

SERVES 6

I sometimes replace the ground hazelnuts with ground almonds, but whichever I use fresh raspberries or strawberries are an ideal accompaniment to this dish. Cream lovers may also like to serve it with a little lightly chilled cream or crème fraîche.

---

3 EGG YOLKS
225 g/8 oz RICOTTA CHEESE, SIEVED
40 g/1½ oz GROUND HAZELNUTS
40 g/1½ oz CANDIED ORANGE PEEL
75 g/3 oz CASTER SUGAR
FINELY GRATED RIND OF 1 SMALL LEMON
2 EGG WHITES, WHISKED

Gradually stir the egg yolks into the ricotta cheese, keeping the mixture smooth. Stir in the ground hazelnuts followed by the candied orange peel, sugar and lemon rind. Lightly fold in the egg whites, then divide the mixture between 6 oiled 150 g/5 oz ramekin dishes. Lay a sheet of foil in the bottom of a steaming basket or on a rack. Place the ramekin dishes on top and steam for 5 minutes. Remove from the heat and leave to stand for a few minutes before turning out on to plates.

WALNUT CAKE

MAKES 1 × 22.5 cm / 9 in RING

The tendency of many ovens to cook unevenly is particularly noticeable when baking delicate cake mixtures. Using a steamer for such mixtures eliminates this problem as the heat rises evenly. If you do not have a steaming basket large enough to take the cake tin, place it on a rack raised above the level of the water (see page 13).

---

3 EGGS, SEPARATED
40 g / 1½ oz SUGAR
40 g / 1½ oz DEMERARA SUGAR
25 g / 1 oz UNSALTED BUTTER, JUST MELTED
115 g / 4 oz WALNUTS, CHOPPED THEN FINELY GROUND
1 TABLESPOON COLD STRONG COFFEE
1 TABLESPOON SELF-RAISING FLOUR

Whisk the egg yolks with the sugars until pale, fluffy and very thick. Lightly fold the butter, walnuts, coffee and flour into the mixture.

In a separate bowl, whisk the egg whites until stiff, but not dry, then lightly fold into the walnut mixture. Spoon into an oiled 22.5 cm / 9 in spring-form ring cake tin, lay a sheet of greaseproof paper on the top then steam, in a steaming basket or on a rack, for 17 minutes, until a skewer inserted into the centre of the mixture comes out clean.

Using the point of a knife, gently ease the cake away from the side of the tin. Leave the cake to stand for a few minutes before removing from the tin and leave to cool on a wire rack.

HONEY AND SAFFRON DESSERTS

SERVES 4

The portions are not large but they are rich and satisfying. Make them in fancy tins of various shapes such as small, fluted tartlet tins. Serve with steamed sliced Cox's Orange Pippins.

FEW STRANDS SAFFRON
2 TEASPOONS MEDIUM-BODIED DRY WHITE WINE
115 g/4 oz DOUBLE CREAM CHEESE
2 TEASPOONS ACACIA HONEY
75 ml/3 fl oz SINGLE CREAM
½ TEASPOON FINELY GRATED LEMON RIND
1 LARGE EGG, BEATEN

Soak the saffron in the wine for 10 minutes. In a separate bowl, mix the cheese and honey together, then gradually blend in the cream and saffron liquid until smooth. Mix in the lemon rind and egg. Pour the mixture into 4 oiled fancy tins, approximately 50 ml/2 fl oz.

Lay a sheet of foil in a steaming basket or on a rack. Place the tins on top and cover with another piece of foil. Steam for 7 minutes, until just lightly set. Remove from the heat and leave to stand for a few minutes.

Carefully run the point of a sharp knife around the top edge of the tins, then turn out. (Don't worry if the surface has a slightly curdled appearance.) Serve while still warm.

MINI SPONGE PUDDINGS

SERVES 4

The basic mixture can be flavoured with whichever two of the flavourings you like – or if you would like to serve all three make 1½ times the quantity (ie 75 g / 3 oz butter, sugar and flour and 1½ beaten eggs) and use a third for each flavouring.

BASIC MIXTURE
50 g/2 oz BUTTER
50 g/2 oz SUGAR
1 EGG
50 g/2 oz SELF-RAISING FLOUR
PINCH OF SALT

Cream together the butter and sugar until pale, light and fluffy, then gradually beat in the egg. When thoroughly mixed in, gently fold in the flour and salt.

TREACLE PUDDINGS
½ OF THE SPONGE PUDDING MIXTURE
APPROX 3 TABLESPOONS GOLDEN SYRUP
CUSTARD, TO SERVE

Butter 8 small moulds and put 1½–2 teaspoons golden syrup in the bottom of each. Divide the sponge mixture between the moulds then steam for about 6 minutes until risen and springy to the touch.

Leave to stand for a minute or so then turn out on to small pools of custard on warm plates.

CHOCOLATE PUDDINGS
½ OF THE SPONGE PUDDING MIXTURE
75 g/3 oz PLAIN CHOCOLATE, BROKEN
APPROX 50 ml/2 fl oz DOUBLE CREAM

Melt 15 g/½ oz of the chocolate in a bowl placed over a saucepan of hot water, then carefully fold into the sponge pudding mixture. When just evenly mixed divide between 8 small buttered moulds, then steam for about 6 minutes.

Meanwhile, melt the remaining chocolate with 40 ml/1½ fl oz of the cream in a small bowl placed over a saucepan of hot water, stirring frequently until smooth.

Turn the puddings out on to warmed plates. Spoon some of the sauce over each one, and place a small blob of the remaining cream on top.

GINGER PUDDINGS
½ OF THE SPONGE PUDDING MIXTURE
SMALL PINCH OF GROUND GINGER
VERY FINELY CHOPPED GINGER PRESERVED
IN SYRUP
LEMON SORBET, VANILLA ICE CREAM, OR CUSTARD,
TO SERVE

Mix the ground ginger into the sponge pudding mixture. Press sufficient very finely chopped ginger on to the sides of 8 small buttered moulds, then fill with the sponge mixture. Steam for about 6 minutes.

Leave to stand for a minute or two then turn out on to warm plates. Serve with lemon sorbet, vanilla ice cream, or on a small pool of custard.

STICKY MARMALADE PUDDING

SERVES 4

To simplify the otherwise tricky job of lifting the pudding basin from the steaming basket once the pudding is cooked, place a long strip of double-thickness foil, about 5 cm/2 in wide, beneath the basin and extending up and over the sides of the steaming basket or saucepan.

---

75 g/3 oz SELF-RAISING FLOUR
¼ TEASPOON BAKING POWDER
75 g/3 oz BREADCRUMBS
PINCH OF SALT
40 g/1½ oz SHREDDED SUET
40 g/1½ oz COLD BUTTER, FINELY CHOPPED
1 EGG, BEATEN
75 g/3 oz CHUNKY ORANGE MARMALADE
APPROX 4 TABLESPOONS MILK
CUSTARD, PREFERABLY HOME-MADE, OR VANILLA
ICE CREAM, TO SERVE

Stir together the flour, baking powder, breadcrumbs, salt, suet and butter, and form a well in the centre. Stir the egg, marmalade and a little milk into the well to make a dough of soft consistency. Transfer to a greased 900 ml/1½ pint pudding basin, cover the top of the pudding with a piece of greaseproof paper, then cover the basin with a piece of foil pleated across the centre and secure with string. Place in a steaming basket or colander and steam for 1½–2 hours, until a skewer inserted into the centre comes out clean. Serve with home-made custard or vanilla ice cream.

SUSSEX POND PUDDING

SERVES 6

Turn the cooked pudding out on to a warmed plate before serving, so that when it is cut, the juices flow out to form a rich golden buttery, lemony pond around the pudding.

---

225 g/8 oz SELF-RAISING FLOUR
PINCH OF SALT
50 g/2 oz SHREDDED SUET
50 g/2 oz COLD BUTTER, COARSELY GRATED
1 TEASPOON FINELY GRATED LIME OR LEMON RIND
1 EGG, BEATEN
50–75 ml/2–3 fl oz MILK
APPROX 150 g/5 oz COLD UNSALTED BUTTER, DICED
APPROX 150 g/5 oz SOFT LIGHT BROWN SUGAR
1 LARGE THIN-SKINNED LEMON

Mix together the flour and salt, then stir in the suet, grated butter and lime or lemon rind and form a well in the centre. Make the egg up to 150 ml/¼ pint with milk, pour into the well then mix in the dry ingredients to form a soft, but not sticky, dough. Turn on to a lightly floured surface, knead gently, then roll out to a 30 cm/12 in circle. Cut out a quarter of the dough in a wedge shape to within 2.5 cm/1 in of the centre. Set aside. Line a buttered 1.5 litre/2½ pint pudding basin with the large portion of dough.

Toss together the diced butter and sugar. Place two-thirds of this mixture in the lined basin. Prick the lemon well all over with a large needle and place on the butter mixture in the basin. Pack the space around the lemon with the remaining butter mixture so that the basin is completely full.

Roll the reserved dough out to a circle, about 2.5 cm/1 in wider than the top of the basin. Dampen the exposed edge of the lining dough. Cover the top of the pudding with the dough circle. Seal the edges together.

Cover the top of the pudding with a piece of buttered greaseproof paper, then cover the basin with a piece of pleated foil. Secure firmly with string.

Lower the basin into a saucepan containing sufficient water to come half-way up the side of the basin. Cover and cook for 2½ hours, topping up with more boiling water as necessary.

INDEX